A Cultural History
of the
United States

∎

Through the Decades

The 1960s

Gini Holland

Library of Congress Cataloging-in-Publication Data

Holland, Gini.
    The 1960s / by Gini Holland.
        p.   cm.—(A cultural history of the United States through
    the decades)
    Includes bibliographical references and index.
    Summary: Discusses the political, historical, and cultural life of
the United States in the 1960s, including the space race, civil rights,
the Vietnam War, and the counterculture as reflected in music and
the arts.
    ISBN 1-56006-556-7 (lib. : alk. paper)
    1. United States—History—1961–1969 —Juvenile literature.
2. United States—Social life and customs—1945–1970 —Juvenile
literature. 3. Nineteen sixties—Juvenile literature. [1. United States—
History—1961–1969. 2. United States—Social life and customs—
1945–1970. 3. Nineteen sixties.] I. Title. II. Series.
E841.H65   1999
973.92—dc21   98-8826
                                                                          CIP
                                                                           AC

Copyright 1999 by Lucent Books, Inc.
P.O. Box 289011, San Diego, California 92198-9011

Contents

Introduction: Invitation to a Revolution:
A Decade of Choice and Change 4

Chapter One: Cold War and the End of Camelot 12

Chapter Two: Guns and Butter: Politics in the 1960s 28

Chapter Three: The Vietnam War and
Johnson's Great Society 39

Chapter Four: Civil Rights: The Quest for Equality 57

Chapter Five: Countercultures Provide Alternatives 79

Chapter Six: Arts and Entertainment
Reflect the Counterculture 92

Chapter Seven: The Space Race and Technology
Take Us to the Moon 111

Notes 123

Chronology 126

For Further Reading 130

Works Consulted 132

Index 136

Picture Credits 143

About the Author 144

Peaceful protests often turned violent, as when these antiwar protesters clashed with military police and U.S. marshals in Washington, D.C., in 1967.

Invitation to a Revolution: A Decade of Choice and Change

The sixties were years of struggle and celebration, a decade of extremes of hope, freedom, joy, and progress in turn with dark tragedy, angry confrontation, and despair. "You better start swimming or you'll sink like a stone, for the times they are a-changin'," singer-songwriter Bob Dylan advised. Choices flooded American society on all fronts: political, social, moral, cultural, scientific, and technological. After a fairly quiet postwar decade, the sixties were years in which change was the only constant. People were forced to examine their most cherished beliefs, their most comfortable traditions, and make choices that would take them to a better social union—or tear society apart.

In choosing left or right, the most extreme right-wing conservatives and extreme leftist liberals rarely saw any way to compromise with one another on the pressing issues of the day. Confrontation was often the result: Conservative segregationists squared off against liberal integrationists over civil rights. Prowar conservatives denounced those against the war in Vietnam as un-American, while antiwar demonstrators tried to end the war through peaceful or sometimes violent confrontations.

The Silent Generation Sets the Stage

In the fifties, the so-called Silent Generation (born between 1925 and 1942) had enjoyed the peace and prosperity that followed the terrors of World War II. Yet, with the end of that war, the nagging threat of nuclear attack caused anxiety for many, fueled by fear of the "Red menace." This fear of communist domination allowed the spread of McCarthyism, an anticommunist campaign named for its main champion, Wisconsin senator Joseph McCarthy.

When McCarthy's ideas and tactics were discredited in the mid- to late

Wisconsin senator Joseph McCarthy vowed to make a clean sweep of the "card-carrying" Communists working in government, but his hearings turned into a witch-hunt.

fifties, most voters remained strongly anticommunist. However, many people began to move away from McCarthy's blind prejudice against left-wing ideas. Concepts of the left, such as populism and socialism, were once again considered in the sixties.

Presidents Resist Pressure to Wage Nuclear War

When the sixties began, the cold war continued with no end in sight. The debate between generals and politicians continued as well. As White House records and transcripts show, U.S. military leaders often advocated the use of nuclear bombs, while both Republican president Dwight D. Eisenhower and Democrat John F. Kennedy wanted to avoid their use, if possible. In late April 1954, some members of the National Security Council suggested the use of atomic bombs on Korea during a meeting with Eisenhower. Eisenhower remembered the horrible atomic bombs dropped on Hiroshima and Nagasaki in Japan. In their book *Where the Domino Fell: America and Vietnam, 1945–1990,* authors James Olson and Randy Roberts report that Eisenhower exploded, "You boys must be crazy. We can't use those awful things against Asians for the second time in less than ten years. My God!"

A celebrated general himself in World War II, Eisenhower left office in 1960 warning against a "military-industrial complex." He saw a powerful alliance between the military and private U.S. industry. This "complex" had a great many weapons and a great deal of money. As such, it held tremendous power.

The military created a demand for guns, tanks, and other military supplies from private industry, making this "war industry" sector of the economy rich with taxpayers' money. This sector could afford to make huge financial contributions to political campaigns. The war industry could make sure that it supported politicians who voted for wars so that the mili-

The thirty-fourth president of the United States, Dwight David Eisenhower served two terms marked by cold war conflicts and increasing civil rights demands in the midst of economic prosperity for middle-class Americans.

tary would have reason to buy their weapons and continue to keep them rich. In this and other ways, the partnership between the military and U.S. industry was seen as a serious and uncontrolled force in American life. The role of the military-industrial complex in the U.S. economy was frequently attacked by antiwar groups throughout the sixties. In naming it and warning against the military-industrial complex, Eisenhower helped set the stage for questioning the Vietnam War and the economic reasons for fighting it.

The New Left Opposes War, Supports Civil Rights

The New Left groups that drove most of the political change in the sixties began as a loose alliance of old socialists and prolabor politicians, joined by civil rights and antiwar activists. They were supported by student groups such as the Free Speech movement, Students for a Democratic Society, and, eventually, the women's liberation movement and groups representing minorities such as Chicanos and American Indians. While these groups often disagreed with one another's tactics and final goals, most came together to oppose the Vietnam War and support both the civil rights movement and civil liberties.

A surprising spirit of playfulness and gentle provocation often found its way into a decade punctuated by assassinations and riots. Yippie cofounder Abbie Hoffman threw money onto the floor of the Stock Exchange and watched the brokers scramble for a buck. Antiwar demonstrators, in a more serious gesture, put flowers in the gun barrels of National Guardsmen.

Those caught in the middle of political and social extremes during this rapidly changing decade often found themselves pulled first in one direction and then the other. In spite of numerous confrontations, the mood throughout much of the sixties was brightened by the sense that, more than ever, Americans had choices. There was no longer only one way to do things, or a single way to look at a problem or find a solution. It was an exciting—although extremely challenging—time to be alive. And through it all, the music was great.

Science and Technology Shake Things Up

In the sixties, Americans wrestled with more than social upheaval. They had to accept a number of technological and scientific changes in daily life, from birth control pills to satellite communications. Television came of age, in color for the first time. The proportion of U.S. households with one or more television sets rose to 75 percent. Televised national and international live news reports made the world seem smaller and more intimately connected than ever before. The "news cycle," or delay between an event and news reports of the event, shrank from days to hours, then to minutes. Live reporting made President Kennedy's assassination and other key events intense and moving experiences for the entire nation.

The Postwar Generation Makes Its Mark

Many of the postwar baby boom generation, faced with the conformist demands and consumer values of their parents, became hippies with a culture of their own. They experimented with communal living, marijuana, and LSD. The anarchist poets and artists of the fifties, known as the Beat generation, acted as elders and guides to this counterculture movement and encouraged rejection of middle-class values.

As the rebellious and playful baby boomers came of age and went to college in the sixties, their energy, style, attitudes, and sheer numbers gave them the power to leave an indelible mark on the decade. The decade, in turn, changed them, showing them the limits of peaceful demonstration and political provocation. Also called the Woodstock generation in honor of their landmark rock festival, these youths questioned authority and tradition. Many refused to go to war, even when drafted. Their favorite music, rock 'n' roll, exploded in variety and complexity and became the dominant art form of the day. Many musicians, from Jimi Hendrix to Country Joe and the Fish, promoted revolutionary change that drove another wedge between the younger and older generations. The dialogue between generations became shrill at times, but out of this intense

From wearing "flower power" clothes to burning draft cards, baby boomers challenged the older generation.

conversation came many of the changes in American life that we take for granted today.

A Democratic Decade Destroyed by Conflict

It was largely a Democratic decade, dominated by liberal ideas in conflict with conservative traditions. With the power of the president's support, the Democratic Party tried to move poor people into the middle class with President Lyndon Johnson's War on Poverty. Democrats championed the cause of civil rights for African Americans, although reluctantly at times. In spite of these positive efforts, the Democratic leadership also found themselves trapped in a war in Vietnam that the United States could not win.

The riots and conflicts that surrounded these changes frightened average Americans enough to vote for a more conservative Republican White House by 1968, in a very close presidential race. Republican Richard Nixon won by just 1 percent of the vote, after segregationist George Wallace captured 20 percent of the vote with his own law-and-order campaign. Controversy about the war was tearing the country apart, and Nixon promised a return to law and order and "peace with honor" in Vietnam. Democratic presidential hopeful Eugene McCarthy had asked "What if they gave a war and nobody came?" Student groups supported him, but they were not strong enough to give him the nomination. The stronger Democratic candidate, Robert Kennedy, running against the war in Vietnam, was assassinated in June 1968. In August 1968, the Democratic National Convention in

Honoring Diversity

The sixties began with increased tolerance, partly as a reaction to the excesses of the 1950s McCarthy era of "witch-hunts" for American communists. McCarthyism had been strongly opposed by the Free Speech movement and by newscasters such as Edward R. Murrow.

One sign of voters' greater tolerance of differences was the election of Kennedy, the first Catholic to be elected president in U.S. history. Another sign of tolerance of those "different" than the average American was that intellectuals were more welcome in Kennedy's White House than they had been under past presidents. Under Kennedy, according to Henry Kissinger, professors for the first time were treated as more than just advisers. They were actually given operational responsibilities. Kennedy's stature as a World War II hero who could be tough with the Soviets encouraged public confidence. It also made Kennedy's more liberal Democratic policies and his promotion of the arts more acceptable to conservatives, and allowed him to inspire youth, minorities, and the poor with his support. The Kennedy White House promoted the arts as government funding for orchestras, opera, ballet, and other fine arts expanded across the country.

Chicago ended in shambles as antiwar demonstrators provoked a police riot. The country watched live television coverage of peace demonstrators beaten and arrested. Partly as a reaction to this collapse of law and order, Americans would elect only one other Democrat, Jimmy Carter, to the presidency in the next twenty years.

The Democratic candidate who survived that disastrous convention, Hubert Humphrey, supported President Johnson's Vietnam War until the last few weeks of the campaign. Nixon, on the other hand, promised he had a "secret plan" to end the war, although it took seven more years to actually get American soldiers out of Vietnam.

The Large Legacy of the Sixties

By the end of 1968, the New Left had many martyrs to its causes: President John Kennedy, Martin Luther King Jr., Robert Kennedy, Malcolm X, and Medgar Evers, head of Mississippi's National Association for the Advancement of Colored People (NAACP), were all assassinated in the sixties. The nation, however, had moved forward rather than strictly left or right. Legal segregation of the races was finally abolished. The civil rights movement pushed the country through what can be described as the last battle of the Civil War, bringing the vote and equal civil rights to millions of African Americans.

Political power and attitudes about war shifted greatly in the sixties. The antiwar movement helped establish voting rights for those old enough to be drafted into the military. For the first time in U.S. history, a war was televised and an antiwar movement became powerful enough to help end it. Because of the lessons learned in that conflict, the U.S. government today prefers more limited military objectives than it set in Vietnam. This influence has been shown in military actions such as the Gulf War and U.S./UN intervention in the civil war in Bosnia.

The legacy of the sixties also continues to be felt in social programs, public policy, and the right to peaceful protest. Medicare and Medicaid programs, Head Start, and other antipoverty programs begun in the sixties established a safety net for the country's poor and elderly that has so far endured. Free speech and the right for peaceful assembly and protest were tested and upheld as basic freedoms in American society. The tactic of nonviolence became a powerful tool for change in a time when violence was all too prevalent.

In this decade of extreme change,

Dr. Martin Luther King Jr. inspires his followers after a civil rights march in Selma, Alabama.

American society struggled to move, not to extremes of left or right, but together toward a future in which all citizens enjoyed equal legal protection, rights, and respect. In so doing, the six-ties helped lay the foundation for the multicultural society in which Americans live today, where change is an accepted—and expected—part of life.

Chapter One

Cuban refugees living in the United States gather around their television as President Kennedy speaks to the nation about Cuba in 1962.

Cold War and the End of Camelot

The cold war that began with the end of World War II emerged from a struggle for power between the United States and the Union of Soviet Socialist Republics that pitted one against the other in a postwar arms race and made them ideological enemies. Although the two nations had been military allies during war in the fight against Nazi Germany, they had widely different forms of government and international political goals. Called superpowers because of their size, influence, and military strength, the United States and the Soviet Union saw each other as threats: Their many political, economic, and social differences created conflicts throughout the 1950s and 1960s.

Most Americans not only viewed the Soviet Union as a political and military rival but also saw Soviet leadership as a brutal and unyielding force. By the time John F. Kennedy was elected president in 1960, many Americans saw Soviet premier Nikita S. Khrushchev as a typical Soviet: aggressive, humorless, overbearing, and given to long and darkly threatening speeches against the American way of life. Despite his now-acknowledged skill as a diplomat and his efforts to create political and economic reforms in the USSR, Khrushchev made a perfect target for those who viewed the Soviet Union as a hungry, menacing Russian bear.

In addition, the United States, with its commitment to democracy and capitalism, strongly opposed the economic and political policies of the Soviet Union, which practiced communism and a totalitarian form of government. The United States and its allies viewed communists as rigid and restrictive: Their economic system did not allow the free market forces of supply and demand to determine the price of goods and services. Instead, under communism, the government set the kinds, quantities, and prices of crops and manufactured goods. Freedom

of religion, free speech, and the right to travel were also severely restricted. Citizens who disagreed with the government were often imprisoned under cruel and harsh conditions.

One belief of communism particularly concerned the United States. The Soviet government believed that communism would inevitably spread worldwide, and that converting the world to that system through international revolution was a moral duty. The

Soviet premier from 1958 to 1964, Nikita Khrushchev declared a policy of "peaceful coexistence" but often confronted the United States in ways that helped bring the two countries to the brink of nuclear war.

Soviet Union's actions during the years after World War II, including its military takeover of Eastern Europe, demonstrated to most Americans that the Soviets would attempt to take over nations by force if necessary.

Believing itself the leader of the free world (those nations free from the totalitarian regimes of Eastern Europe and the Soviet Union), the U.S. government made opposing communism one of its fundamental foreign policy goals. Officials in the United States hoped that, by supporting noncommunist countries, they would be able to extend the U.S. "sphere of influence," those countries that responded favorably to U.S. power and influence politically, economically, or militarily. The United States wanted to maintain a strong network of friendly countries in hopes that, in times of crisis, these nations would help the United States.

Nuclear Standoff

Both the United States and the USSR had nuclear weapons, but their battleground became the fight for control of world economic and political systems, rather than all-out war. Since such a war would inevitably bring about untold destruction, nuclear bombs were

considered a "mutual deterrent," or the kind of weapon that neither side wanted to fire, for fear the other would strike back with the same deadly force.

In the early sixties, Americans were especially worried about the threat of nuclear war, with good reason. Soviet missiles armed with nuclear warheads were pointed at the United States and Europe; the United States, for its part, aimed nuclear missiles at the Soviet Union. Each side had enough weaponry to destroy the human population of the world many times over. Nuclear bombs could destroy lives and cities the way conventional, or nonatomic, weapons could, only on a larger scale. In addition, nuclear fallout could wither crops and poison the planet and its inhabitants. Unlike conventional bullets and explosives, atomic weapons could also cause cancers and radiation sickness in many survivors.

Held in check by these atomic dangers, both sides were nevertheless willing to do almost anything short of nuclear war to gain advantage over the other. For each side, the key to waging a successful cold war was knowing when to advance and when, strategically, to retreat. The many diplomatic skirmishes and military standoffs that took place were designed to advance each side's political, economic, and military sphere of influence.

Hot Spots in the Cold War

One of the most serious crises of the cold war took place in 1960. The Soviet Union shot down a U.S. U-2 spy plane on May 1. Although both countries routinely spied on each other throughout the cold war, their leaders had always denied espionage activities and claimed to object to spying on principal. Soviet premier Khrushchev was no exception.

Immediately after the U-2 capture, U.S. president Dwight D. Eisenhower claimed he knew nothing about it. Eisenhower said the U-2 was doing weather research and had accidentally strayed off course. U.S. advisers had told him it would be safe to maintain this position because the pilot could not have survived the landing. However, as historian Michael Beschloss relates:

> On May 7, Khrushchev dramatically contradicted Eisenhower's claims when he told a full session of the U.S.S.R.'s legislature, the Supreme Soviet, "Comrades, I must let you in on a secret. When I first made my report two days ago, I deliberately refrained from mentioning that we have the remnants of the plane—and we also have the pilot, who is quite alive and kicking!"

"We did this quite deliberately, because if we had given out the whole story, the Americans would have thought up still another fable. And now, just look how many silly things they have said: . . . scientific research and so on. . . . The pilot's name is Francis Gary Powers. He is thirty years old. He says he is a first lieutenant in the U.S. Air Force, where he served until 1956—that is, until the day he went over to the Central Intelligence Agency."[1] Gary Powers was indeed a spy, taking aerial photographs of Soviet military installations.

This incident forced Eisenhower to admit that the American government did, indeed, practice espionage, an unprecedented admission. Khrushchev was furious. He also knew how to use his anger to good political advantage. In his usual dramatic way, he warned, "Our country is a strong and mighty state. . . . If the U.S.A. has not yet suffered a real war on its territory and wants to start a war, we will fire rockets and hit their territory a few minutes later. . . . We do not live under American laws. We have our own laws. . . and violators will be thrashed!"[2] Having expressed his outrage over the incident, Khrushchev then demanded an apology from the United States. President Eisenhower responded by stopping all U-2 flights over the Soviet Union. Khrushchev accepted this ges-

The capture of U-2 pilot Francis Gary Powers (pictured) angered Soviet premier Khrushchev so much that the U.S. defense secretary put American military forces on full alert.

ture, but he let it be known that the Soviet Union was still angry. When Eisenhower refused to apologize, Khrushchev walked out of the May 16 Paris summit conference between the Soviet

Union, Great Britain, France, and the United States. Eisenhower had hoped this conference would be the crowning achievement of his presidency.

The next day, Khrushchev declared that unless Eisenhower apologized he would return home. The summit crumbled, and Eisenhower returned home without his much-hoped-for agreement to ban tests of nuclear weapons. Gary Powers was sentenced to ten years in prison, but he was set free two years after he was shot down, in exchange for convicted Soviet spy Rudolph Abel.

Trying to Free Cuba from Communism

The serious threat of nuclear war, coupled with the absence of a test ban treaty that might have halted or slowed the development of nuclear weapons, intensified political anxieties in the United States. Some government leaders supported the idea of limited military actions against communist nations. One of these nations was Cuba, under the leadership of Fidel Castro, the revolutionary leader who on January 1, 1959, had led a revolution to topple dictator Fulgencio Batista y Zaldívar.

The Soviets proved more welcoming than the United States to the new revolutionary leadership in Cuba, and when Castro responded by embracing

communism, the United States feared a new and uncomfortably close threat to its sphere of influence. Americans worried that Castro, who now received diplomatic and economic support from the USSR, would allow the Soviets to establish a military presence in Cuba and encourage other nations in Central and South America to rebel against their own governments, many of which were supported by the United States.

Revolutionary hero-turned-premier of Cuba, Fidel Castro took property and businesses from wealthy Cubans and turned his country into a communist state.

Even more frightening to many Americans was the possibility that the Soviet Union, now allied with a nation some ninety miles off the coast of Florida, might be able to place nuclear weapons within easy striking distance of the United States. Cuba's proximity, many feared, would give the Soviets a first-strike capability against the United States. First strike means launching nuclear weapons against an enemy first, destroying the enemy's ability to strike back. Many feared that a preemptive Soviet missile launch from Cuba would be disastrous. Thus the prospect of Cuba remaining under communist leadership posed both a political and a military problem for the government of the United States.

President John F. Kennedy, guided by his military advisers, believed a military takeover to overthrow Castro was necessary. Kennedy staged a surprise invasion of Cuba on April 17, 1961, by Cuban exiles trained and paid by the U.S. government and living in the United States. The invasion failed on the beaches of Cuba's Bay of Pigs. The U.S.-backed troops were killed or cap-

tured, and the United States suffered an embarrassing defeat. Internationally, the U.S. government was seen as an intruder into the affairs of a neighboring sovereign nation, with whom it had started an unprovoked confrontation. On the home front, this image was aggravated by the fact that a U.S.-backed military operation against a small foe had resulted in such complete failure.

The Wall Goes Up

The U.S. government attempted to isolate Cuba from all nations throughout North and South America by setting up a trade boycott and cutting off diplomatic relations. Meanwhile, the Soviets supported Cuba and continued to consolidate Soviet power in Eastern Europe. In 1961, for example, Khrushchev ordered a fortified, guarded wall built between East and West Berlin. This German city, divided into sectors by the occupying powers that had defeated Germany in World War II, was surrounded by Soviet-controlled East Germany, and, as such, was a focus of ongoing power struggles throughout the cold war. By August 13, 1961, the border between Communist-controlled East Berlin and free West Berlin was closed.

In October 1961, Khrushchev decided to test the United States by increasing Soviet control of this border. He ordered Soviet and East German guards to make U.S. officials show their passports at "Checkpoint Charlie" when they crossed into the eastern part of the city.

Kennedy responded by sending U.S. National Guard and reserve troops, totaling around fifteen hundred men, into West Germany. After a tense sixteen-hour standoff between armed Soviet and U.S. tanks at Checkpoint Charlie, Khrushchev ordered a retreat.

Cuban Missiles and Nuclear Threats

The most severe cold war battle of Kennedy's administration came in 1962. This time, the question was

Symbols of the Cold War

The Berlin Wall was seventy miles long and protected by thirty thousand armed Soviet and East German troops. East Berliners who tried to cross over the wall to get to their families, neighbors, and freedom on the other side were summarily shot. The wall on the Communist-controlled side was painted white in order to make easy targets of people trying to escape.

For President Kennedy, and for people throughout the world, the divided city of Berlin was a living symbol of the cold war. The wall did not come down until 1989, but when it did, Berliners celebrated in the streets, pulling down the bricks and drinking champagne over the rubble because, with the wall down, they were free, they were no longer divided, and the cold war was effectively over.

American soldiers guard the west side of the Berlin Wall in 1961, unable to help East Berliners leave the communist side of their divided city.

not simply whether the United States would protect Western Europe. The question was, could the United States protect itself?

On October 22, 1962, Kennedy put the United States on military alert after the Central Intelligence Agency (CIA) suspected that the Soviet Union was storing forty offensive missiles, all armed with nuclear warheads, in Communist Cuba. Construction of a launch site was underway. Once the missiles were installed, Cuba's proximity to the United States would put the nation in danger of immediate attack.

In addition to their concern over the threat posed by nuclear missiles in Cuba, some of Kennedy's advisers worried about the moral responsibility of the United States in the face of nuclear war. Attorney General Robert Kennedy, the president's brother, pointed out that starting a nuclear war was a moral issue that determined what kind of country America was. Both men knew that if they started a nuclear war, they risked destroying or crippling life on earth,

Aerial photos convinced President Kennedy that offensive nuclear missiles had been brought into Cuba by the Soviet Union. This photo, taken by a high-altitude spy plane, shows a nuclear missile site under construction.

marking Americans with a shame they could never erase.

In dealing with what became known as the Cuban missile crisis, Kennedy had three tasks: to prevent nuclear war, to remove the immediate threat of nuclear missiles off the coast of Florida, and to remain in charge of his military advisers. Some of them thought a nuclear war was coming, no matter what, and that this would be a good time to "get it over with." Kennedy did not agree. He had learned his lesson with the Bay of Pigs disaster. Kennedy cautioned an aide to make sure the U.S. military stationed in Europe, especially in Turkey and Italy, did not take matters farther than he wanted them to go, saying, "We may be attacking the Cubans, and a reprisal may come. . . . We don't want these nuclear weapons firing without our knowing it."[3]

Nuclear Overkill

On August 6, 1945, one atomic bomb had been enough to level 90 percent of the Japanese city of Hiroshima and kill 130,000 people. By 1962 the United States was capable of launching 2,000 atomic weapons—less than a tenth of its total force—at the Soviet Union on a moment's notice. The Soviet Union had only about 340 atomic warheads ready to strike the United States, but that would be more than enough to, as some described it, "blast the United States back to the Stone Age," meaning that the country would no longer have such basic comforts of civilization as electricity, running water, transportation, telephones, central heat, or modern agriculture. Bombing the Japanese cities of Hiroshima and Nagasaki with two atomic bombs had effectively ended World War II. By the time the Cuban missile crisis occurred, the United States and the Soviet Union had

On August 9, 1945, Nagasaki, Japan, was hit by the second atomic bomb ever exploded on a populated area. It destroyed one-third of the city, killing or injuring over seventy-five thousand people.

enough atomic bombs to possibly end civilization itself.

Naval Blockade Helps Diplomacy Work

On the edge of nuclear war, Kennedy worked carefully. On October 22, he addressed the American people on television about the nuclear missiles and promised that the United States was monitoring construction in Cuba closely. If the installation was continued, the United States would take further action. He did not spell out what that action would be.

The next day, with official approval of the Organization of American States (OAS), an international organization of many countries in the Western Hemisphere, Kennedy announced a Proclamation of Quarantine. He set up a naval blockade to keep Soviet military ships from entering Cuban waters. He hoped to demonstrate U.S. military strength but give both sides time to try diplomacy, winning with words what could not be won with weapons. He began to work with Khrushchev, the United Nations Security Council, and the North Atlantic Treaty Organization (NATO), a regional defense alliance of European nations, the United States, and Canada. NATO had been formed in 1949 to address the fear of Soviet military domination in Europe.

Cuba Cut Off from Its Neighbors

The Organization of American States, or OAS, is an international organization that works with the United Nations to peacefully promote economic development in the Western Hemisphere. It also promotes justice, solidarity, sovereignty, and the territorial integrity of its member nations. It was founded on April 30, 1948, in Bogota, Colombia, by the following countries: Argentina, Bolivia, Brazil, Chile, Colombia, Costa Rica, Cuba, the Dominican Republic, Ecuador, El Salvador, Guatemala, Haiti, Honduras, Mexico, Nicaragua, Panama, Paraguay, Peru, the United States, Uruguay, and Venezuela.

Cuba was formally expelled from the OAS in 1962, charged with attempted subversion of other OAS countries. The member countries of OAS began a trade boycott of Cuba two years later, and ended diplomatic relations with the communist country. However, most Latin American countries resumed trade and diplomatic relations with Cuba by the 1990s, abandoning the United States, who continues the boycott alone. Some practical results of this boycott have been a shortage of new cars, machinery, and many medicines in Cuba. It has also contributed to much illegal smuggling, especially of prized Cuban cigars. Travel to Cuba from the United States continues to be prohibited in most circumstances, and the United States does not have an embassy in Cuba.

Fortunately, Khrushchev did not want a nuclear war any more than Kennedy did. On October 28, after public words and private letters, Kennedy and Khrushchev ended the missile crisis with an agreement, and the missiles were dismantled and withdrawn.

Hope and Patriotism Flourished

In spite of the escalating dangers of the cold war and the threat of nuclear destruction, Kennedy helped Americans feel hopeful during his presidency. An effective and charismatic speaker, Kennedy inspired people to give more to their country. During his inaugural address in 1961 he asked people to think about helping the country and the world at large, saying, "Ask not what your country can do for you—ask what you can do for your country."[4] As the youngest man ever to be elected president, Jack Kennedy brought youthful good looks, wealth, culture, class, and many of his handsome family members to the job. His brother Ted was elected to fill the president's former Senate seat, representing Massachusetts. This gave the president a strong connection in the Senate. He appointed his younger brother Robert, called Bobby, to be his attorney general.

The president's strongest political asset might have been his wife, Jackie. Unlike most political wives, Jacqueline Bouvier Kennedy knew Washington well, even before she moved her young children, Caroline and John Jr., or John-John, into the White House. Jackie had been a socialite news photographer, covering the Washington scene, before she married Jack. She understood how Washington worked. She had also been a debutante, raised with wealth, and was used to high society. She was beautiful, intelligent, a devoted mother, and she seemed more like a gracious queen than a president's wife. As such, she won many admirers throughout the world. President Kennedy seemed to enjoy her popularity, and he smiled when he introduced himself to the French press, explaining, "I'm the man who accompanied Jackie to Paris."

Many minorities, especially African Americans, felt they had the president on their side in the Kennedy White House. Under the president's brother Bobby, the Justice Department listened and answered African Americans' pleas for fairness and equal treatment under the law. Yet President Kennedy often stopped short of signing laws that would put the force of federal laws behind civil rights for blacks. Finally, when Governor George Wallace of Alabama gave in at Tuscaloosa on June

President Kennedy enjoyed strong support from black voters, who felt he explained their concerns to the nation.

11, 1963, and let two black students register at the segregated University of Alabama, Kennedy decided to ask Congress to write a law that would be called by many "the Second Emancipation Proclamation." He announced his intention to the nation at large, saying, "One hundred years of delay have passed since President Lincoln freed the slaves, yet their heirs, their grand-sons, are not fully free. Now the time has come for this nation to fulfill its promise. We are confronted primarily with a moral issue. It is as old as the scriptures and it is as clear as the American Constitution."[5] He sent a bill to Congress that asked for an end to discrimination in all public accommodations, public education, and voter registration.

Many African American families hung President Kennedy's picture next to their framed portrait of civil rights leader Dr. Martin Luther King Jr. They believed these two leaders were going to make a difference for their people.

Civil Rights

Harris Wofford, President Kennedy's special assistant for civil rights, worked hard to get the president to create new civil rights laws. Wofford met frequently with civil rights leaders, and urged them to meet with the president so that Kennedy would hear their concerns firsthand. Wofford had also helped Martin Luther King get a formal invitation to India, urging him to learn and use Gandhi's tactics of nonviolence. Yet when the March on Washington and time for presidential action finally came, Wofford was far away, helping Sargent Shriver run the Peace Corps. In his memoir, *Of Kennedys and Kings: Making Sense of the Sixties,* he remembers the politics behind the dramatic scenes, and how close in time so many of these events truly were:

At first the President thought the proposed March on Washington would antagonize Congress, but in an encounter with King, A. Philip Randolph, James Farmer, and others, he finally agreed—and said publicly—that it was in "the great tradition" of American protest. . . . On August 28, 1963, when Kennedy met the leaders at the end of the massive, triumphant march, he greeted them with King's refrain, "I have a dream."

At the American Embassy in Addis Ababa, I watched a special film of the March with a group of Peace Corps and Ethiopian friends of Ambassador Edward Korry. Again I felt the awful frustration of distance as we saw a quarter of a million people, black and white together, moving down the Mall, through the heart of Washington to the Lincoln Memorial.

Two weeks later a bomb killed four little girls attending Sunday school in Birmingham's Sixteenth Street Baptist Church. Again the President spoke strongly to the nation. . . .

On November 21, as Kennedy was leaving for a visit to Texas, the news came that the bill—stronger than any that had ever passed Congress—had been reported favorably out of the House Judiciary Committee and was ready to be sent to the floor by the House Rules Committee. In his last press conference before the trip, a high-spirited Kennedy gave his judgment that "by the time this Congress goes home" a civil rights bill—along with measures on education, health, and taxes—would be enacted. "However dark it looks now, I think that 'westward, look the land is bright,' he said, and predicted that "by next summer it may be."

The next day, President Kennedy was murdered. His hope for light winning over darkness was not fulfilled in his lifetime.

The End of Innocence

On November 22, 1963, however, hope and innocence began to crumble. Many Americans vividly remember where they were, and what they were doing, when they heard the news.

It was such a sunny day that President Kennedy, in Dallas, Texas, for a scheduled speech, asked to ride in an open car. With the plastic bubble removed, he and Jackie waved to the waiting crowds as their convertible moved slowly through downtown Dallas. Suddenly, at about 12:30 P.M., two shots rang out. Kennedy and Texas governor John Connally were hit. Connally was seriously wounded, but he survived. The president suffered grave head and neck wounds; moments later he was dead.

Vice President Lyndon Johnson, concerned that the Soviets might have been behind the assassination, considered the possibility of nuclear attack, since the United States was momentarily without a president and therefore without a commander in chief who could order a counterattack. He wanted to get airborne, for safety's sake. Aboard the president plane Air Force One, Johnson was sworn in as president of the United States, with his wife, Lady Bird Johnson, standing on his right, and Jackie Kennedy, suddenly a widow, on his left. That afternoon, she had held her dying husband in her arms. Now she had to return to Washington to bury him.

Most Americans reacted with grief and anguish on behalf of Kennedy's wife and family. As the reality of his death hit home, the public increasingly felt the loss of its chief executive, its commander in chief, and the bright promise of the presidential administration that had come to be known as Camelot.

For days, the mourning nation watched television in a kind of national vigil. Public schools were closed, as were most businesses. Newscasters soberly covered the events that followed the president's death on live television. On Sunday, November 24, the networks broadcast the transfer of Kennedy's alleged assassin, Lee Harvey Oswald, from his jail cell in the basement of the Dallas police station. He was twenty-four years old, a Dallas resident who had lived for a while in the Soviet Union. Official and unofficial reports speculated that he was a Communist spy.

As millions of viewers watched, Jack Ruby, a local nightclub owner in the crowd of spectators, pulled out his gun and shot Oswald dead. The president's accused murderer was himself murdered on live television.

Doubts and Distrust Increase

Oswald's death made his trial an impossibility and fueled an enormous body of anti-Castro Cubans living in the United States, still angry about Kennedy's refusal to invade Cuba a second time? Was it President Johnson, who might have stood to gain, or perhaps the Republican Party? Few believed the wild theories that prompted these questions, but it was hard to make sense of what had happened.

Two things were clear: The president was dead, and the president's accused murderer had been killed on live television. In fact, according to FBI director J. Edgar Hoover, Oswald had been moved during the day, rather than during the relative safety of night, to give the television crews enough light. Thus began an era of televised trauma that would grow worse with the Vietnam War.

Hardest of all for the country, in the long run, was the way mistrust now seemed to grow. The president's murder in Dallas had shaken Americans' faith. There seemed to be evil forces at work, and no one would take the blame. Many Americans' lack of trust would increase as the government continued its policies in Southeast Asia. Many would begin to wonder, "What are we fighting for?" Clear answers would prove hard to find.

Jack Ruby fatally shot Kennedy's alleged assassin, Lee Harvey Oswald, leaving many questions about the president's murder unanswered.

conspiracy theories and questions of motive. Only two bullets were fired from Oswald's gun, and both had hit the president. So who shot Governor Connally? Who was really behind the assassination? Was it the Communists? Was it

Chapter Two

On June 18, 1968, the Poor People's March in Washington, D.C., emphasized economic links to racism, crime, and other national problems.

Guns and Butter: Politics in the 1960s

When he stepped into President Kennedy's office, Lyndon Baines Johnson tried to revive the optimism that seemed to have died with the assassinated president. Kennedy had been working on an antipoverty program in the fall of 1963, and Johnson decided to make it a cornerstone of his administration. In January 1964 he announced that he would begin a "War on Poverty." He promised to put the late president's programs into law, and began to lead the country out of mourning with a vision of what the country could be; what he called the Great Society. The laws and programs that resulted from this vision would be his legacy to the nation.

Johnson found he had to balance two major components of the economy:

28

military needs and social programs. Economists often describe this as a problem of "guns or butter," since most countries cannot afford to supply both at the same time.

First World War II, then conflicts in Korea and Vietnam, made the U.S. government a major purchaser of military supplies. The "war sector" of the U.S. economy was also supported by countries who bought American military hardware to provide for their own security. The manufacture of weapons and other instruments of war provided high-paying jobs for workers and huge profits for many U.S. companies.

Butter: Feeding Middle America

With the economy strengthened by military spending, Johnson convinced Congress to pass an $11 billion tax cut in January 1964, which left the middle and upper classes with more spendable income. Now they were able to purchase more goods and services. Nonmilitary factories and businesses began to fill this consumer demand, which further strengthened employment and wages.

Tax cuts did not help the poor directly, since they had so little income on which they paid taxes. But a strong economy meant that the United States might now afford to face some of the social issues connected with poverty

that had been neglected for generations. As president, Kennedy had pointed out that, although they lived in the richest country in the world, 17 million Americans went to bed hungry every night. In the early sixties, half of the poor were not yet in cities, but remained scattered in rural areas. By targeting the poor, Johnson helped make them more visible.

Fighting the Causes of Poverty

On May 22, 1964, Johnson explained his Great Society agenda for the first time, telling a new generation of college students at Ann Arbor, Michigan, "In your time we have the opportunity to move not only toward the rich society and the powerful society, but upward to the Great Society." In this speech, Johnson promised to organize White House conferences and meetings to deal with poverty, urban blight, and education, declaring that "The Great Society rests on abundance and liberty for all."[6]

Johnson saw racism as an important cause of poverty, since racism often meant fewer jobs for blacks than whites, as well as inferior education and less pay for equal work. The civil rights movement, led by Dr. Martin Luther King Jr. and others, was pressuring the nation to change the way blacks were treated. Johnson supported their cause by making civil rights for all

Americans a top priority of his administration. He linked civil rights to his War on Poverty and his hope for a Great Society.

The connection between race and poverty was a simple fact: In 1959, the average black wage earner made about $3,419 a year, compared to $4,198 for the average white wage earner. Black heads of households were paid, on average, $2.00 an hour compared to $2.32 for white heads of households.

Blacks also were given fewer hours of overtime, which further limited their earning power. The unemployment rate was much higher among blacks than whites.

These were the average workers. The truly poor, both black and white, were much worse off. As Vice President Hubert Humphrey explained:

In the midst of our rich society there is an "other America." There are some 30 million Americans in

Johnson, the Conservative Liberal

A congressman since 1937, Johnson had an unusual political record that mixed liberal and conservative policies. To help Texan farmers, Congressman Johnson had supported such liberal government programs as power projects built with federal aid, rural electrification, Social Security, and farm price supports. To please his more conservative supporters, and to help the business community, Johnson had also supported efforts such as limiting the power of unions, which represented the working man, or labor. While he was a congressman, Johnson had counted heavily on the votes of both farmers, who often wanted government tax dollars to help them out, and businessmen, who typically wanted the lower taxes and low minimum wage that would keep their costs down.

Johnson was known as a "country liberal." This image gave him a unique ability to persuade more conservative members of Congress that he used common

sense, "country" values when it came to matters of race relations and other controversial issues. Many conservatives trusted him because, early in his career, as a typical Texan in those times, he tended to side with the South on civil rights. For example, Johnson consistently voted against bills that tried to outlaw lynching, a practice of mob murder often used against blacks, saying in 1948 (as Ronnie Dugger noted in "The Johnson Record—II" published in the *Texas Observer*, June 10, 1960), "I am opposed to the anti-lynching bill because the federal government has no more business enacting a law against one form of murder than another." As a senator, Johnson also voted repeatedly to keep the poll tax, which was one of many methods southerners used to keep blacks from voting. Yet, as president, the historic civil rights act was enacted with his strong support, in part because many southern legislators trusted him as "one of them."

it. They have been shunted aside or lost in the backwaters. For them our national prosperity is something seen but seldom shared. These Americans belong to families earning an average $1,800 a year from all sources. That is $35 a week—to feed that family, to clothe that family, to house that family, to provide education and transportation and health care for that family.[7]

Humphrey also pointed out the costs of poverty to the nation:

The costs of welfare are a continuing drain on American communities. The "other Americans" are tax eaters and not taxpayers. There are estimates which indicate that hundreds of millions of dollars each year could be added to our economy; that hundreds of millions of dollars could be subtracted from our public budgets through greater investment to break the "other Americans" cycle of poverty.[8]

Johnson wanted to change the factors that fed the cycle of poverty and drained the nation economically and socially. He asked the Michigan students—and youth around the country—to fight a war at home:

So, will you join in the battle to give every citizen the full equality which God enjoins and the law re-

quires, whatever his belief, or race, or the color of his skin? Will you join in the battle to give every citizen an escape from the crushing weight of poverty? . . . Will you join in the battle to build the Great Society, to prove that our material progress is only the foundation on which we will build a richer life of mind and spirit?[9]

Johnson Achieves Landmark Legislation

In the summer of 1964 (the summer before his election), Johnson successfully pushed three landmark pieces of legislation with the help of the Democratic majority in Congress. Together they passed the Civil Rights Act of 1964 in July, the War on Poverty Act on August 11, and the Economic Opportunity Act on August 20, which provided funding and direction for the War on Poverty agencies.

The historic Civil Rights Act outlawed many methods used to keep African Americans from voting, such as unfair reading tests. It also outlawed the common practices of refusing to serve African Americans in restaurants, gas stations, hotels, motels, and places of amusement. It barred discrimination under any program that received federal money and authorized the attorney general to

Money and Programs Fight Poverty

President Johnson signs the Civil Rights Bill he helped move through Congress.

Johnson also persuaded Congress to fund the War on Poverty at over a billion dollars, more than ten times the Peace Corps allocations under President Kennedy. The Economic Opportunity Act created the Office of Economic Opportunity to coordinate and direct the many government and private agencies that were fighting poverty. On October 8, 1964, Congress provided the Office of Economic Opportunity with $800 million in federal funds to support such programs as Head Start, Job Corps, and VISTA, among others.

Johnson saw these programs as his major weapons in the War on Poverty. His Job Corps provided residential living and job training for youth between ages sixteen and twenty-two who were not in school and who were from impoverished families. The Neighborhood Youth Corps encouraged participants to stay in school while they were given job training, and the College Work-Study

prosecute school desegregation suits and cases involving the Fourteenth Amendment to the U.S. Constitution.

Program funded part-time employment for college students from low-income families.

VISTA, or Volunteers in Service to America, created a domestic Peace Corps for poor neighborhoods throughout the United States. On the first anniversary of the War on Poverty, Humphrey reported that

> VISTA has already attracted the volunteered service of more than 20,000 Americans of all ages, of all backgrounds, and from all parts of our land. The first 1,000 of our Nation's finest citizens are now on the job or in training—in Appalachian hollows, on Indian reservations, in urban and rural slums. By the end of the year they will number 2,000—working in 40 states.[10]

The idealism of the young VISTA volunteers was tested constantly. They lived in the poor neighborhoods they served, and many attempted to politically organize the poor so that they would have a voice in local and national decisions that affected them. This did not always meet with support from local politicians, who often felt threatened by local community organizers and consequent increased political power of the poor.

Some charged that the programs were poorly managed, and listed instances of waste, abuses, and trading of political favors. Sargent Shriver and Hubert Humphrey, the general coordinators of the War on Poverty program, defended it, saying that it had made significant progress and would strengthen the United States economically.

Education: A Way to Escape Poverty

Johnson reasoned that better education can lead to better-paying jobs, and can help people work their way out of poverty. He had decried the quality of the country's educational system, saying, "Most of our qualified teachers are underpaid, and many of our paid teachers are unqualified. So we must give every child a place to sit and a teacher to learn from. Poverty must not be a bar to learning, and learning must offer an escape from poverty."[11]

Education for rural blacks, especially poor blacks, had been underfunded and substandard for generations, partly because public education is largely paid for through property taxes, so richer communities pay more taxes and therefore spend more money per pupil than do those in poor communities, in the absence of supplemental federal funds.

Since parents are key teachers for young children, it made sense to create federal programs that would support

The Invisible Face of Poverty

In political science classes across the country, college students of the 1960s were reading such books as J. K. Galbraith's *The Affluent Society* and Michael Harrington's *The Other America,* first published in 1962. President Kennedy also read Harrington, and was impressed. These authors developed the idea that poor people were becoming "invisible" in the United States at a time when most were becoming richer. They maintained that the poor were being ignored, suffered silently, and needed government help.

For many members of the affluent baby boom generation, the courses they were taking in college showed them the problems that poor people in the country were facing, and encouraged them to try to do something about it. In his 1969 edition of *The Other America,* Harrington took a hard look at what government had done to end poverty. He showed how some government programs actually made poverty worse. For example, federal subsidies paid to corporate farmers allowed them to mechanize their farms so they did not need as many farmhands. This forced the corporate farmers' farmhands out of their jobs and off the land. These farmworkers went to the cities to find work, but most did not

Author Michael Harrington's book on Americans in poverty influenced Presidents Kennedy and Johnson.

have the skills to land jobs that paid well. Harrington pointed out that, unlike the huge number of workers who became poor when they lost their jobs during the Great Depression of the 1930s, the poor in the sixties were more scattered, and therefore usually lacked political clout.

As many others had done, Harrington showed how racism created a high poverty rate for blacks. He also stressed the connection between poverty and government support for big business and agricultural corporations. He reported that "between 1950 and 1966, Federal monies thus helped to force 5.5 million black farm workers into the cities. They came from areas where education for Negroes was substandard and they were required to relate to a bewildering, complex urban environment and compete in a sophisticated labor market."

Now these people often seemed to be a burden to the average taxpayer. Harrington argued that the real source of the problem was the federal policy to pay billions to the agricultural rich in such a way as to exile the poor from the land. Under Kennedy and Johnson, the federal government was listening to Harrington's point of view. It was starting to pay attention to "the other America."

those parents who grew up in poverty and thus had likely received a poor education themselves. Preschool education programs such as Head Start were intended to enrich the early learning experiences of poor children to give them the same "head start" that children from richer communities had always received. Head Start would also provide food and health care to preschoolers, to help attack the health and nutrition causes of the poverty cycle.

Having achieved legislation for education, job training, and civil rights, Johnson began to give elderly voters his attention. He convinced Congress to pass a historic Medicare bill, which he introduced on July 1, 1966, that provided medical benefits to persons over sixty-five. Unfortunately, this and other government "entitlement" programs began to cost taxpayers a great deal of money. The number of elderly was increasing, and so was the cost of health care. This combination helped to earn Johnson and many future Democrats the label "tax-and-spend liberals."

Even the elderly used tactics of nonviolence in the sixties, including these protesters during a demonstration for Medicare on August 26, 1964.

Legislative Action Was Johnson's Legacy

With his superior persuasive and political skills, Johnson was able to achieve what Kennedy, in his brief presidency, could not: legislation that made a significant difference to the nation. Kennedy had been able to get an aid-to-depressed areas bill, known as the Area Redevelopment Administration, through Congress on May 1, 1961. He also achieved the Accelerated Public Works Act of 1962, which increased federal money for public works projects. Both bills were designed to improve unemployment, and they did provide some direction to reduce poverty. In comparison, many of Johnson's programs, from Head Start to Medicare, were larger and broader in scope. They have provided services and influenced society from the sixties to the present.

Johnson's accomplishments did not end with his first term. While he was president, more bills were passed into law than at any time since President Franklin Delano Roosevelt's New Deal legislation that helped poor people during the Great Depression of the 1930s. As many have described, Johnson could twist the arms of congressmen better than most: One contemporary described him as a politician who "took to the techniques of influence and pressure like a kitten to a warm brick."[12] With his support for civil rights and antipoverty programs, real change was on the way. The question was, would the American public accept these changes?

The Great Society Leaves Its Mark

Johnson hoped that by improving civil rights, medical care, and jobs the cycle of poverty would be broken and his Great Society could flower. Unfortunately, with each passing year, the Vietnam War bled more of the nation's resources. Less and less money was available for Johnson's Great Society programs; nevertheless, these programs made a significant difference. The poverty rate was cut in half during this decade, falling from 22 percent in 1959 to 12 percent in 1969. The Civil Rights Acts of 1964 and 1965 gave equal rights to all Americans, regardless of race, setting a standard of fair treatment for the nation. This, combined with the War on Poverty Act and the Economic Opportunity Act, would prove to have a large impact not only on the economic health of the nation, but on the social climate of the country for decades to come. With these programs many Americans, and especially black Americans, began to hope for a better life.

The Race, Education, and Poverty Connection

In the South all citizens, black and white, paid taxes for white schools, which were heated and lit with that tax money. But schools for black students did not receive as many tax dollars, and the black communities often had to pay for heat and electricity for their own schools out of their own pocket, without the help of the taxes they paid. Many students throughout rural America, black and white, only attended school during the winter months, when the harvest was in and before spring planting had begun. The "invisible poor" in the countryside usually had no way to get as much money or as much education as their peers in the cities. In *RFK Collected Speeches,* editors Edwin O. Guthman and C. Richard Allen provide some background for Kennedy's speeches, noting:

> There were many voices speaking out against poverty. They tried to tell middle class and upper class Americans about the tragic lives, largely invisible, that the poor were living while most Americans enjoyed the best economy in the world. They also tried to speak about some of the causes, including business practices of mining companies and others, the dislocations of workers as the economy changed, and the failure of government and citizens to provide a good safety net—insurance, benefits, a living wage, retraining—for workers whose jobs were lost. In a speech he intended to deliver at Kansas State University in February 1968, summarizing his experiences in Mississippi, Rochester, and Delano, Robert Kennedy wrote: "in this richest of nations, we have allowed the perpetuation of poverty and degradation which can only be described as outrageous. In the ghettos of the great cities are hundreds of thousands of men without work.". . .

> And there are others: on the back roads of Mississippi, where thousands of children slowly starve their lives away, their minds damaged beyond repair by the age of four or five; in the camps of the migrant workers, a half million nomads virtually unprotected by collective bargaining or social security, minimum wage or workman's compensation, exposed to the caprice of fate and the cruelty of their fellow man alike; and on Indian reservations where the unemployment rate is 80 percent, and where suicide is not a philosopher's question, but the leading cause of death among young people. Only a minority are poor. But poverty affects all of us. . . . The facts of poverty and injustice penetrate to every corner, every suburb and farm in the nation. Their existence is the message of every evening news broadcast, crippling our satisfaction in our ownership of one, or two, or three, of American's seventy million television sets. . . .

> Our ideal of America is a nation in which justice is done; and therefore, the continued existence of injustice—of unnecessary, inexcusable poverty in this most favored of nations—this knowledge erodes our ideal of America, our basic sense of who and what we are. It is, in the deepest sense of the word, demoralizing—to all of us.

The Price of Change, the Costs of War

Johnson would find, however, that the cost of the war in Vietnam, in both dollars and lives, would prove too great for the nation, both economically and socially. Even the richest country in the world could not easily afford both the "butter" to uplift its poor and the "guns" needed to win this war. For many of the generation that had to fight it, and for their parents who paid the bills, the cost in lives and dollars seemed too much to bear. The war in Vietnam would gradually overshadow Johnson's efforts to build a Great Society.

Yet perhaps the greatest cost of the decade was the social upheaval that came from so much change combined with strong disagreement about this war. For some, too much change came too fast. For those who were poor and discriminated against, on the other hand, social and economic changes often felt long overdue. Arguments raged over issues from foreign war to civil rights to taxpayers' responsibility for the poor. Many prayed for peace, but few found it during the sixties.

Chapter Three

The South Vietnamese army faced the impossible job of fighting communism while supporting the corrupt South Vietnamese government.

The Vietnam War and Johnson's Great Society

Just as Kennedy had turned to the nation's youth to volunteer for his international Peace Corps, Johnson looked to the baby boom generation to support his War on Poverty and drive toward a Great Society. In general, the baby boom generation was not only the largest but, on average, the richest and the most educated generation America had ever produced. These youths went to college in record numbers in the sixties, in large part because the National Defense Education Act of 1958 provided tuition help just when more

youth came of college age than ever before. Accordingly, attendance in institu-
tions of higher learning increased
eightfold, from around a million in
1950 to around 8 million by the end of
the sixties.

Addressing this generation directly
in his Ann Arbor speech, Johnson told
them:

> For better or for worse, your gener-
> ation has been appointed by his-
> tory to deal with those problems
> and to lead America toward a new
> age. You have the chance never be-
> fore afforded to any people in any
> age. You can help build a society
> where the demands of morality,
> and the needs of the spirit, can be
> realized in the life of the nation.[13]

As the decade unfolded, this generation did challenge the prevailing
moral attitudes about war, patriotism,
sex, drugs, racism, and poverty, among
many issues. To the dismay of many,
they did not always agree with their elders. They may have been "appointed
by history," but they did not unques-
tioningly follow the historical leaders of
the day, Johnson included. Because
they were a larger group than any previous generation, baby boomers had a
strong impact on any cause for which
they worked, and their questions and
actions ultimately made a tremendous
difference to the nation. When they

asked baby boomers to work for
change, their elders often ran the risk
of getting more than they bargained for.

The Baby Boom Generation Challenges the War

Ironically, the more they learned at college, the more many students began to
question the government that was
funding their education with government loans. Some of the students at the
Ann Arbor campus had greeted Johnson's Great Society speech with protests
against American involvement in Vietnam. Within a year of his speech, the
students at Ann Arbor began the national teach-in movement to present alternative views to the American public
about what was happening in Vietnam
than were being advanced by government sources. Ann Arbor, along with
universities as different from one another as Berkeley in California and the
University of Wisconsin at Madison,
became strong centers of antiwar ac-
tivism.

The Vietnamese Point of View

Students and many journalists found
that most Vietnamese saw the war as a
struggle for self-determination and
freedom from foreign control. The
French had ruled the region since they
had captured the Vietnamese city of
Saigon in 1859. After the French-

Revolutionary liberator Ho Chi Minh (pictured) was considered the father of his country by most Vietnamese.

into communist and non-communist countries, with communist leader Ho Chi Minh ruling in the north. By the end of that war, at the invitation of the French, the United States was paying about 80 percent of the costs to fight Ho Chi Minh. This committed the United States financially, although not yet militarily, to the region.

Thus the United States found itself supporting a corrupt government in the south, headed by Ngo Dinh Diem, who came into power in 1955. He censored newspapers, accepted bribes, ordered mass arrests of his enemies, and enforced a harsh rule over his people. Naturally, he had little public support. Many South Vietnamese soldiers were therefore less committed to the war than were North Vietnamese soldiers, whose leader, Ho Chi Minh, was a victorious hero against French colonialism.

Diem had promised a 1956 election to unify the country, but canceled it, with U.S. support, because he was afraid that Ho Chi Minh would win in

Indochina War (1946–1954), a 1954 peace agreement separated Vietnam the south. From this point on, it was impossible for the United States to claim that it was fighting for democracy. Without free elections, the most the United States could claim was that it fought communism.

Domino Theory Drives U.S. Policy

The U.S. military had the strong support of those who saw Vietnam as a "domino" that could tip the rest of Asia into communist hands. The domino image was first used at an April 7, 1954, press conference by President Eisenhower, who explained: "You have a row of dominoes set up and you knock over the first one, and what will happen to the last one is the certainty that it will go over very quickly. . . . The loss of Indochina will cause the fall of Southeast Asia like a set of dominoes."[14] Since neighboring communist China and the Soviet Union supplied money and weapons to the North Vietnamese, the United States supported South Vietnam in line with cold war foreign policy.

National History Is No Help

The United States made the mistake of looking to its own history, rather than the history of Southeast Asia, to understand how to win this war against communist North Vietnam. American superior technology, firepower, and the ultimate killing tool, the atomic bomb, had helped win World War II. U.S. strategy in Vietnam was to use a similar approach: saturation bombing and high technology, including chemical warfare with such substances as napalm, a flaming gel developed during World War II, which was sprayed from planes onto enemies and innocent civilians alike. Napalm maimed and killed by burning the skin.

But the United States now faced very different conditions of war in Indochina than in World War II Europe, including guerrilla warfare, a tropical monsoon climate, and a civilian population that was sympathetic to the Vietcong, or North Vietnamese communist guerrillas. The targets of guerrilla attacks were roads, factories, railways, and often, Vietnamese homes. Therefore, the U.S. fight against the communists from the north often became a fight against citizens of the south who were Vietcong sympathizers. It was hard to tell who was the enemy, and many innocent civilians were caught in the crossfire.

Inheriting a War

President Kennedy had inherited the undeclared war in Vietnam from President Eisenhower. In the first days of Kennedy's administration, the Vietcong

Foretelling the Future

Although he authorized aid and military advisers in Vietnam, President Eisenhower seemed to have no great designs on the region and no master plan beyond containing communism. A great general in World War II, he foresaw the problems that could occur if the United States became militarily involved in the region. James Olson and Randy Roberts, in *Where the Domino Fell: America and Vietnam, 1945–1990,* quote Eisenhower saying he "could conceive of no greater tragedy than for the United States to become involved in an all-out war in Indochina."

began sneak attacks on American bases. Without asking Congress to officially declare war, Kennedy increased the number of advisers and sent helicopters and weapons into the region.

Disillusioned by the corruption of South Vietnam's President Diem, the United States began to take covert action, organized within the CIA, to topple him. Diem was executed on November 2, 1963, after a military coup backed by the CIA removed him from power.

Now Johnson, in his turn, inherited the undeclared war. Without congressional approval, the war in Vietnam was illegal, according to the Constitution. Yet Congress found it difficult to declare war against a country that was not di-

rectly threatening the security of the United States. As commander in chief of the armed forces, Johnson was in an awkward position, legally, morally, and politically.

An Undeclared and Undemocratic Conflict

War protests increased across the United States as many questioned the legality of fighting an undeclared war. Many also opposed supporting a government that refused to hold democratic elections, saying that this was fighting not for democracy but for hypocrisy.

Finally, on August 7, 1964, the U.S. Senate passed the Gulf of Tonkin Resolution at Johnson's request, after two American ships in the Gulf of Tonkin were reportedly attacked by North Vietnamese forces. This resolution allowed the president to legally order military strikes in Vietnam. Some disputed this justification, since enemy ships were never verified to be in the area, which had been buffeted by bad weather. Yet at least on paper, there was now some legal justification for the war.

Doves Against Hawks: The Antiwar Movement Grows

By lowering taxes and making progress on poverty and civil rights, Johnson impressed voters and beat Republican senator Barry Goldwater of Arizona, a strong "hawk," or prowar presidential candidate, in a landslide victory in the election of November 1964. Johnson had run effective television adds that hinted that he was working for peace, a "dove" who would both avoid nuclear war and pull back in Vietnam. Within

months of his victory, however, in February 1965, Johnson ordered intense bombing of the north. He was afraid that the communists were going to overrun South Vietnam.

Public support withered. Many began to protest the war, first in letters to their congressmen, then in candlelit marches, and then, as the war went on, in large street demonstrations throughout the country and in the nation's capital. Religious organizations and student groups such as Students for a Democratic Society (SDS) began to actively question the domino theory. Many began to look more critically at America's role in international affairs, and its role in this war in particular.

Bringing the War Home "Live and in Color"

New technology made a difference in how people perceived the war in Vietnam. Satellite television transmission, new in the sixties, brought the war into living rooms "live," or within a few hours of events. In color for the first time, the evening news was suddenly more intense than it had ever been. Satellite technology, coupled with advances in the processing of Kodak color film, made international news seem more vivid—and more urgent—than it had ever been.

News broadcasts showed many people, including innocent civilians, being killed every day. Unlike World War II, which was reported on the radio and in newspapers, the war in Vietnam was being brought right into people's living rooms, nightly, in color. This made the ugly side of war, the horrible death and destruction of innocent men, women, and children, much more real to the American public than in previous wars.

At the same time, cable television was not yet in widespread use. This meant that most communities received news from only three major national commercial networks: NBC, CBS, and ABC. This combination of the three-network system, coupled with new satellite communication, created an unprecedented common experience for the country. Similarly, the world community saw news segments from American and foreign journalists simultaneously, with unprecedented immediacy.

Farmers Caught in the Crossfire

The land of Vietnam is fertile and rich, and farming had been the main occupation of the Vietnamese for centuries. Rice was their chief crop, for which they had constructed an elaborate system of irrigation canals and dikes. In the 1960s over 12 million gallons of the chemical herbicide Agent Orange were sprayed over the forests and farmland of Vietnam, wiping much of it clean of vegetation and causing long-term damage to the soil. The war destroyed many peasant farmers' way of life and they flooded into the cities when land destruction and heavy fighting forced them off their land.

Fear of political and religious persecution from the communists also caused many Vietnamese to leave their homes. After the partition of their country into communist North Vietnam and non-communist South Vietnam, some 900,000 Vietnamese fled to the south. These were mostly Catholics and Buddhists who feared religious persecution by the communists, and others who did not like the communist land reform plans of Ho Chi Minh.

The Whole World Is Watching

On August 3, 1965, for example, the first time that U.S. troops set a Vietnamese hamlet ablaze, CBS's Morley Safer was there to film it for broadcast on the evening news, shocking millions of Americans at home and people around the globe. Some of the most dedicated soldiers of the war were appalled as well. Lieutenant Colonel John Paul Vann wrote at the time, "If this is to be our policy, then I want no part of it and will not be associated with such an effort."[15] For those seeing it in the comfort of their American living rooms on a summer night, the contrast between their lives and the lives being destroyed in Vietnam was extremely upsetting.

Innocent women and children were indiscriminately murdered alongside Vietcong soldiers in May 1968.

One of the most influential newscasters of the time was CBS news anchor Walter Cronkite. When he spoke out against the war on national television, President Johnson himself lost hope of maintaining public support. Johnson despaired, saying that if he had lost Walter Cronkite, then support for the war was over, because he had lost "Mr. Average Citizen."

Live reporting had such strong impact on the public that it began to shape the way demonstrators staged events. Groups and individuals consciously manipulated both television and print media, creating dramatic "demonstrations" to get their point across. These ranged from serious acts of sabotage, such as destroying military draft files, to often humorous but effective street theater, including the Youth International Party (Yippie) manifesto that urged people to protest the next presidential election, in which both major-party candidates supported the war in Vietnam. Yippie founders Jerry Rubin and Abbie Hoffman wrote:

Come into the streets on Nov. 5, election day. Vote with your feet.

Trusted television anchor and reporter Walter Cronkite talks to soldiers in Vietnam on February 28, 1968, and tries to discover what is truly happening in the war.

Rise up and abandon the creeping meatball! Demand the bars be open. Make music and dance at every red light. A festival of life in the streets and parks throughout the world. The American election represents death, and we are alive.[16]

TV coverage brought world scrutiny to bear on abuses of power in Vietnam and at home, and eroded public support for the war. This was especially true at the Democratic National Convention of August 1968, where the crowds chanted "The whole world is watching!" when the Chicago police clubbed and beat antiwar demonstrators. International news was indeed covering this part of the American presidential election process, live. The whole world saw both the vast number of protesters and the violence the Chicago police used to try to stop it. To many, it looked like the United States was being ripped apart.

The Generation Gap Becomes a Gulf

The antiwar movement grew to historically large proportions over the Vietnam War, partly because the sheer number of baby boomers coming of age in the sixties meant that there were large numbers of energetic youths available for both the war and the antiwar movement. Arguments between prowar and antiwar factions polarized families, pitting fathers against sons, brother against brother.

But many in the older generation began to listen to youth protests of the war, and debate on U.S. policy in Vietnam reached the U.S. Senate. Senators J. William Fulbright, Frank Church, and others began formal hearings on the war in 1965. Worried about their antiwar opinions, President Johnson asked the FBI to follow these senators and monitor their activities. He also ordered a wiretap on the office phone of his own vice president, Hubert H. Humphrey. An atmosphere of distrust grew between those who supported the war and those who opposed it. To some, simply questioning the war seemed unpatriotic. This gave rise to the right-wing, or ultraconservative, slogan, "My country right or wrong."

Since many of those against the war were of college (and military draft) age, a popular liberal slogan of the times was "Don't trust anyone over thirty." Certainly, it was men under thirty who would pay the highest price if the United States continued the war. Some young men protested by illegally burning their draft cards. Others fled to neighboring Canada or other foreign countries. Many were caught and jailed. Most of these young men were old enough at age eighteen to be drafted, but too young to vote for or against the war they were being asked to fight. Lacking a vote, they made their opinions heard in other ways. The voting age was changed

Forced to sign up to be drafted for a war they believe is wrong, these young men burn their draft cards on the steps of the Pentagon and face arrest.

from twenty-one to eighteen in 1971 by the Twenty-sixth Amendment, after voters objected to the unfairness of this kind of age discrimination throughout the sixties.

"Credibility Gap" Strains Belief, Destroys Respect

In addition to the so-called generation gap, the media began to describe what it tagged the credibility gap, that is, the difference between what the U.S. government was saying about the war and what was true and credible. For example, by 1967 the Vietcong actually controlled most of South Vietnam, but Johnson claimed the Vietcong ruled only about 20 percent of the south. This gap between government "facts" and the truth did much to destroy public confidence in the war effort. To many voters, Johnson and his military spokespersons began to sound like liars.

Respect for Johnson shifted to disdain. Some citizens began to question all sorts of authority, asking, "Who's really in charge and what do they want? What is this military industrial complex that we pay taxes to support, buying bombers and nuclear warheads, tanks and ammunition? Do we want to keep living in a war economy? Do we want these jobs and profits when our product is war and death?"

Radical Antiwar Actions

When the political process seemed unresponsive to calls to end the war, radical groups formed to protest in new ways. Many attempted to both hurt the military-industrial establishment and call attention to the link between American corporate profits and the war. For example, a group calling itself

Vietnam Veterans Speak Out Against the War

Possibly the most important voice against the war came from Vietnam Veterans Against the War. One of the most powerful speakers from this group was John F. Kerry, a Yale graduate and former navy officer with combat experience in Vietnam. By age twenty-seven, he had received three Purple Hearts, a Bronze Star, and a Silver Star. As a VVAW spokesman, he summed up the lessons of the Vietnam War and the sixties when he spoke to the Foreign Relations Committee of the U.S. Senate on April 22, 1971. He argued for immediate withdrawal from Vietnam. Will A. Linkugal reprints his speech in *Contemporary American Speeches:*

> We saw first hand how money from American taxes was used for a corrupt dictatorial regime. We saw that many people in this country had a one-sided idea of who was kept free by our flag, as blacks provided the highest percentage of casualties. We saw Vietnam ravaged equally by American bombs as well as by search and destroy missions, as well as by Vietcong terrorism, and yet we listened while this country tried to blame all of the havoc on the Vietcong.

> We rationalized destroying villages in order to save them. We saw America lose her sense of morality as she accepted very coolly a My Lai [site of the massacre of Vietnamese villagers by U.S. troops] and refused to give up the image of American soldiers who hand out chocolate bars and chewing gum. We learned the meaning of free fire zones, shooting anything that moves, and we watched while America placed a cheapness on the lives of Orientals. We watched the U.S. falsification of body counts, in fact, the glorification of body counts.

> Each day . . . someone has to give up his life so that the United States doesn't have to admit something that the entire world already knows, so that we can't say that we have made a mistake. Someone has to die so that President Nixon won't be, and these are his words, "the first President to lose a war."

President Johnson encourages his troops in 1966. Despite Johnson's efforts, voter support withered as the war worsened.

the DC 9 targeted Dow Chemical, which manufactured napalm. This company, which actively recruited workers on college campuses across the country, was the focus of antiwar protests from many groups throughout the war. In an open letter addressed to the corporations of America, the DC 9 wrote:

Today, March 22, 1969, in the Washington office of the Dow Chemical Company, we spill human blood and destroy files and office equipment. By this action, we condemn you, the Dow Chemical Company, and all similar American Corporations.

We are outraged by the death-dealing exploitation of people of the Third World, and of all the poor and powerless who are victimized by your profit-seeking ventures. Considering it our responsibility to respond, we deny the right of your faceless and inhuman corporation to exist:

You, corporations, who under the cover of stockholder and executive anonymity, exploit, deprive, dehumanize and kill in search of profit;

You, corporations, who contain (or control) Americans and exploit their exaggerated need for security that you have helped create;

You, corporations, who numb our sensitivity to persons, and capitalize on our concern for things.

Specifically, we warn you, Dow Chemical Company, that we will no longer tolerate your refusal to accept responsibility for your programmed destruction of human life.

You, stockholders and company executives alike, are so willing to seek profit in the production of napalm, defoliants, nerve gas, as in the same spirit you co-operated with the I. G. Farben Company, a chemical manufacturer in Nazi Germany, during the Second World War.

You, who without concern for development for other nations or for their rights of self-determination, maintain 100% control over subsidiaries in more than twenty nations.

You, who in the interest of profits, seek to make it in the military interest of the United States to suppress the legitimate national desires of other peoples. Your product is death, your market is war.

Your offices have lost their right to exist. It is a blow for justice that we strike today.

In your mad pursuit of profit, you and others like you are causing the psychological and physical destruction of mankind. We urge all to join us as we say "no" to this madness.

Statement of the DC 9[17]

In contrast to this strong illegal action, the antiwar movement often used humor as well. One famous example was "levitating the Pentagon," a 1967 event dreamed up by Yippie Jerry Rubin. He convinced antiwar demonstrators to surround the Pentagon, which houses the U.S. Department of Defense, and chant "until it levitates." The five-sided building never flew, but attention was focused on this site of war plans and power,

Bringing the War Home

In addition to targeting Dow Chemical for making Agent Orange and napalm for the army, antiwar activists began to focus on companies that had enjoyed monopolies for decades, such as Bell Telephone and General Electric. These were seen by antiwar activists as part of the military-industrial complex, and therefore part of the problem. Their offices were sometimes physically attacked during antiwar demonstrations. Bricks were thrown through their windows as antiwar demonstrators became more violent and some adopted the tactic of "bringing the war home."

and its nonviolent nature was in keeping with the goal of ending the war.

The War Destroys Johnson's Presidency

In the course of his presidency, Johnson increased the troops in Vietnam from twenty thousand to over five hundred thousand. The war cost more every year, in both money and young lives. Trying to minimize loss of American lives, Johnson increasingly depended on aerial bombing as the war went on, since such air strikes incurred fewer casualties than fighting on the ground with foot soldiers. Yet the body count continued to climb. By 1967 the United States had dropped more

bombs on the tiny country of Vietnam than the combined Allied total during World War II. The destruction of Vietnam was horrific, but North Vietnam was not defeated.

The public wanted an end to this disaster. By the next election, even many in the mainstream of the Democratic Party were voting against the war and for peace candidate Senator Eugene McCarthy, who took delegates away from Johnson in the Democratic primary in New Hampshire.

The war continued to rage. The Vietcong and North Vietnamese regulars had launched the Tet offensive on January 30, 1968, named in honor of the Vietnamese New Year. At this point in Johnson's administration, many of his domestic goals had been realized. Poverty had been reduced and civil rights, although an ongoing struggle, were supported by laws on the books and upheld in the nation's highest courts.

Unfortunately, peace was nowhere in sight—in Vietnam or at home. The antiwar movement was getting louder and angrier, and the civil rights movement suffered church burnings and murders. The country was convulsed in struggles that would either give birth to a better, more peaceful and fair nation or end with the death of Johnson's dream of the Great Society. Baby boomers and others who had accepted his challenge to end poverty and build that society also helped unleash a cycle of dramatic struggle and change that was full of conflict.

Robert Kennedy Challenges Johnson

On March 16, 1968, John F. Kennedy's brother Robert Kennedy announced his candidacy for the presidency. Kennedy had begun to speak out against the war from his seat in the Senate. On March 2, 1967, he told a crowded Senate chamber:

> All we say and all we do must be informed by our awareness that this horror is partly our responsibility; not just a nation's responsibility but yours and mine. It is we who live in abundance and send our young men out to die. It is our chemicals that scorch the children and our bombs that level the villages. We are all participants. To know this and feel the burden of this responsibility is not to ignore important interests, not to forget that freedom and security must, at times, be paid for in blood. Still, even though we must know as a nation what it is necessary to do, we must also feel as men the anguish of what we are doing.[18]

On March 16, 1968, Robert Kennedy declared his presidential candidacy, saying, "At stake is not simply the leadership of our party, and even our country. It is our right to the moral leadership of this planet."

Antiwar demonstrators throughout the country heckled Johnson in public, chanting, "Hey, Hey, LBJ, how many kids did you kill today?" Many in the peace movement flocked to Bobby Kennedy, who promised an end to the war and violence, saying, "The issue, therefore, is how we can serve at once the interest of our country and the most compassionate cause of humanity—the common cause of peace."[19]

Kennedy was passionate on the subject of Vietnam. On March 2, 1967, he told a crowded Senate chamber that Vietnam was a country

> where hundreds of thousands fight, but millions more are the innocent, bewildered victims of brutal passions and beliefs they barely understand. To them peace is not an abstract term describing one of those infrequent intervals when men are not killing one another. It is a day without terror and the fall of bombs. It is a family and the familiar life of their village. It is food and a school and life itself.[20]

Three months after the beginning of the Tet offensive—and just weeks after Kennedy announced his candidacy—Johnson limited the bombing of North Vietnam and surprised the nation on March 31, 1968, with the announcement that he would not seek, nor accept, his party's nomination for reelection. Worn down by antiwar protest, the unwinnable nature of the war, and lack of popular support at home, Johnson was a strong politician defeated by foreign, domestic, and generational conflict.

In June, Kennedy won the California primary that made him the Democratic Party's front-runner. He greeted cheering supporters with a brief victory speech, stepped away from the microphones, and was fatally shot by a Palestinian immigrant among the crowd, Sirhan Bishara Sirhan.

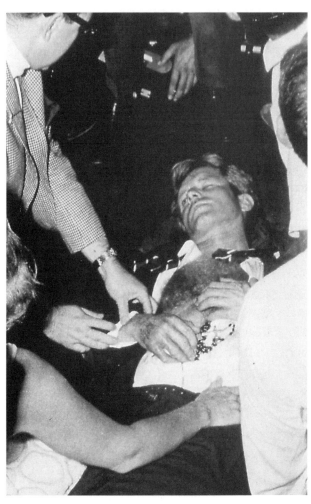

Robert Kennedy lies dying, shot while surrounded by his supporters on June 5, 1968.

The assassin's suggested motive was to protest Kennedy's support of the State of Israel. Many felt that some person—or group—did not want Kennedy, a charismatic peace candidate, to win. The country went into deep mourning as Bobby Kennedy was buried at Arlington National Cemetery next to the grave of his brother, assassinated just five years before.

Nixon Makes a Comeback

Democratic presidential hopeful Hubert H. Humphrey remained loyal to Johnson's war policies, while Republican candidate Richard M. Nixon played on the country's need for a return to law and order after the spring assassinations and the riots at the Democratic convention in August. Nixon easily defeated Humphrey in November. The decade began with Nixon losing to John Kennedy, but ended with both John and Robert Kennedy dead and Nixon occupying the Oval Office of the White House.

During his campaign, Nixon had promised that he had a "secret plan" to end the war. After he was elected, he began what he called "Vietnamization" of the war, a process of gradually withdrawing American troops while South Vietnamese forces took over more and more of the fighting.

But Nixon did not want to become the first American president to lose a war. Soon he widened the war, without congressional approval, to attack communist hideouts in Cambodia, Vietnam's western neighbor. Ironically, Nixon not only became the first president to lose a war, he narrowly escaped impeachment by resigning over his role in the illegal break-in of Democratic headquarters in the Watergate Hotel and subsequent coverup. He did, however, achieve what three previous presidents had been unable to manage: eventual withdrawal from Vietnam.

Fifty thousand Americans died in that war, but the Vietnamese people paid an even higher price: four hundred thousand South Vietnamese and an estimated nine hundred thousand North Vietnamese were killed by the war's end. The country was formally reunited under communist control in July 1976, and Saigon, the South Vietnamese capital, was renamed Ho Chi Minh City. The United States learned many lessons from Vietnam that have shaped foreign policy ever since. Military intervention requires clearer, much more limited objectives than the vague goal of "fighting communism," and the United States has been in general much less willing to police the world.

Chapter Four

Answering Dr. King's call, thousands join the nationally televised March on Washington on August 28, 1963, to demonstrate for racial equality.

Civil Rights: The Quest for Equality

Although the struggle for equal civil rights for all races has marked every decade in the history of the United States, the sixties were years in which the struggle intensified. In this decisive decade, the civil rights movement evolved from isolated though significant court cases and individual acts of courage to mass demonstrations, voter registration drives, and deep changes in the attitudes of many Americans. Civil rights protests often turned into violent confrontations as racist Americans tried to prevent blacks from making progress.

The Journey of One Hundred Years

The shift from three hundred years of slavery to full civil rights did not happen overnight, nor even in the one hundred years since the Civil War (1861–1865). On the contrary, the beginning of the centennial remembrance of that war, in 1961, found African Americans only partly free. African Americans were free from slavery, but not yet free to go to any public school, shop in any store, or ride on any seat of a public bus. Throughout most of the United States, blacks lived in segregated neighborhoods and communities. In many places in the South, they were not allowed to use "white" water fountains, restaurants, or restrooms, or wait in the "white side" of the train or bus station.

Legal Second-Class Citizenship

Segregation was maintained in the South by Jim Crow laws, first written in the 1880s. These laws legalized segregation of blacks and whites. They were upheld by the Supreme Court's *Plessy v. Ferguson* ruling of 1896, which declared that separate facilities for blacks and whites were constitutional. Racial bigotry, social custom, and obstacles to education and jobs also helped enforce the status of African Americans as second-class citizens for the next hundred years.

In many communities in the South, discriminatory local and state restrictions kept African Americans from even registering to vote. With sole political power, whites could pass laws that not only kept African Americans socially oppressed, but also without a fair chance in the job market. As a result, many lived in extreme poverty, with poor nutrition and inadequate medical care.

White Judges Enforce Federal Integration Laws

Federal legislation in the midfifties had begun to uphold the rights of African Americans, opposing individual state laws that still enforced racial segregation. Although African Americans had a difficult time voting, they were able to sue for their rights in court. In *Brown v. Board of Education* (1954) the Supreme Court declared that "separate but equal" schools and public facilities were unfair, unequal, and, most importantly, unconstitutional throughout the entire United States. This ruling was made in a case brought by the parents of Linda Brown, who had been denied admission to her local school in Topeka, Kansas, because she was black.

The *Brown v. Board of Education* ruling meant that African Americans had, for the first time, a legal civil right to attend any public school. Equally important, it also implied that they had a legal right to patronize any public building, park, or facility, and be served in the same manner as anyone else. Unfortunately, *Brown v. Board of Education* was not enforced in most communities until federal troops oversaw mandated integration on campuses across the South.

Equal Education Means Integrated Education

African Americans were ready to act on the Supreme Court's support for integrated education. But white segrega-

The Brown v. Board of Education *decision gave legal support to these first black and white students who had the courage to integrate public schools.*

tionists were quick to fight these legal changes. For example, in Louisiana, on December 1, 1960, white students began a school boycott when the first black students enrolled. Most white parents kept their children home rather than have them sit in the same classroom with black children.

Many southern politicians took dramatic steps to support segregation. Governor George Wallace personally barred the doorway to keep African American students from entering the University of Alabama. Although Wallace apologized years later, and said he was wrong to stand in the way of progress by black Americans, in the sixties Governor Wallace and others led many conservatives in a fight against civil rights for blacks.

Facing Danger and Death

In spite of danger from white resistance, blacks of all ages began to register at all-white schools and insist on their right to an equal education. In 1962, James Meredith became the first black student to enroll at

James Meredith (center) claims his legal right to enroll at the University of Mississippi on October 1, 1962.

the University of Mississippi. It took three thousand federal troops to put down the riots that followed. Meredith came to symbolize the power of an individual act of courage, and of the tremendous opposition often faced by those who tried to obtain their legal rights for equality. He did not stop at claiming his right to integrated education. After he became the first black graduate of the University of Missis-sippi, he tried to claim the right of African Americans to move freely in the South by making a highly publicized one-man "Walk Against Fear" from Memphis, Tennessee, to Jackson, Mississippi. Deep in racist country, he was shot and wounded by a sniper on the second day of his journey. The American public was outraged, and thousands of blacks and whites joined together to finish the march for him.

President Johnson ordered federal agents to hunt for his attacker. From this and other demonstrations met by violence, people around the United States began to see how intensely segregated the South really was, and how far segregationists were willing to go to keep African Americans in the position of second-class citizens.

Nonviolence: A Tool for Change

Individual acts of defiance that gained attention in the fifties gathered tremendous support in the sixties when integrating not only schools but any public facility. For example, in 1959, during the last year of the Eisenhower administration, four black college students sat down at a Greensboro, North Carolina, lunch counter. They were denied service, but they refused to move. In the months that followed, others began to "sit in" at other lunch counters throughout the South. By September 1961, some seventy thousand black and white protesters had joined the sit-in movement. Guided by the nonviolent principles of civil rights leader Dr. Martin Luther King Jr., they practiced a very special, and highly effective, method: passive resistance, or nonviolent civil disobedience.

King had studied the Indian political and spiritual leader Mahatma Gandhi's nonviolent methods to win freedom for the people of India. Ironically, Gandhi first developed his pacifist approach in racially segregated South Africa, where he used it to oppose the strict segregation practices called apartheid. He was able to achieve an agreement with the South African government that promised to stop anti-Indian discrimination. Gandhi went on to promote nonviolence so effectively in India that he is credited with freeing India from British colonial control in 1947.

Nonviolence Becomes a Civil Rights Weapon

Passive resistance, or the use of nonviolence, is a way of standing one's ground without fighting back or violently resisting arrest or attacks. It requires great self-discipline and courage. It is also a powerful tool for change. King made nonviolence a cornerstone of his civil rights movement, and began to share Gandhi's ideas whenever possible. According to Taylor Branch: "On summer break in 1961, King had visited Lawson and other Freedom Riders [civil rights workers dedicated to testing integration] imprisoned at Parchman Penitentiary, smuggling to them the gift books by Gandhi concealed within Billy Graham jacket covers."[21]

In promoting nonviolence, King raised the civil rights movement to high moral ground and kept it there.

Choosing Tactics

The Congress for Racial Equality, or CORE, a civil rights organization that actively practiced nonviolent demonstration techniques, grappled with the growing call to violence. In 1965, James Farmer, national director of CORE, wrote in *Freedom— When?* "We must show that non-violence is something more than turning the other cheek, that it can be aggressive within the limits a civilized order will permit. Where we cannot influence the heart of the evil-doer, we can force an end to the evil practice. Boycotts, picketing, civil disobedience, unflinching courage, and brute persistence are virile enough for any man whose aim is to accomplish something. Even professions of love have a forceful effect at times. Gandhi himself said that he would prefer to see a man resist evil with violence than fail to resist evil out of fear. The choice therefore is not at all between pure love and violence. Between them there are many paths which are psychologically valid and politically effective."

He forced people to focus on issues of fairness and justice, jobs and freedom, rather than on fighting or fighting back. If they practiced nonviolence, civil rights demonstrators could not be criticized for poor behavior. Demonstrators would not fight the police, but they would not cooperate with them, either. Police had to drag civil rights protesters into the police vans. Pictures of this passive resistance, in the newspapers and on television, helped emphasize the justice of the civil rights cause. The more civil rights demonstrators resisted peacefully, the more sympathy they received. In contrast, segregationists who attacked them appeared cruel and unreasonable.

King Inspires the Nation

King's work gained national attention beginning with the Montgomery, Alabama, bus boycott, sparked by Rosa Parks when, while riding a bus, she refused to give a white man her seat in 1955. King became the boycott's most articulate spokesperson and helped achieve national attention and support. The black community of Montgomery walked to work for almost a year, refusing to ride the buses. Ultimately, King and the Montgomery Improvement Association (MIA) filed suit with the Supreme Court, which ruled that Montgomery had to integrate its buses. It did so on December 21, 1956.

A majority of Americans already believed, as the U.S. Constitution states, that "all men are created equal." Martin Luther King's "I Have a Dream" speech, televised live across the nation from the March on Washington, August 28, 1963, inspired many, both black and white, to seek equality for all. King found an audience, both in

The "Mother of the Civil Rights Movement"

Rosa Parks turned a single act of courage into a spark that ignited the Montgomery bus boycott. By the time she met Martin Luther King in 1955, she was already working for African American civil rights. She was the secretary of the Montgomery branch of the National Association for the Advancement of Colored People (NAACP) in 1943, and tried for the next two years to register to vote in her community. In 1945 her persistence paid off, and at age thirty she was allowed to vote for the first time in her life.

A police officer fingerprints Rosa Parks after she is arrested on a city bus for refusing to give her seat to a white man.

Then, on December 1, 1955, not long after she met King, she paid the same ten-cent fare as all the other passengers on her bus, both black and white, and sat down in the "colored" section at the back of the bus. When a white man got on, there were no more seats in the "white" part of the bus. The white driver told Parks to give the white man her seat. She refused, and was arrested. She was tried, found guilty of breaking one of the many Jim Crow laws enforced in the South at that time, and sent to jail on December 5.

But she was not alone. Most of the black community rode the bus to work in Montgomery. Without their bus fares, the bus company would go broke. To protest their treatment, the majority of black riders stopped taking the bus. They got up early and walked. They carpooled. They rode bicycles. They stayed off the Montgomery city buses for over a year. When the Montgomery city buses were integrated, some segregationists tried to smear the reputations of Rosa Parks and Dr. King. Some even paid for a billboard in Alabama that showed a picture of Martin Luther King, Rosa Parks, and others under the false banner: "Martin Luther King at Communist Training School." This was, of course, a lie aimed at painting civil rights activists as un-American.

the over two hundred thousand black and white demonstrators who joined him in the March on Washington, and in the millions who watched this historic march on television, who were ready to listen and be deeply moved by what he had to say. The marchers walked from the Washington Monument to the Lincoln Memorial. Ten civil rights leaders, including King, met with President Kennedy and then returned to address the crowd.

The most often quoted words from King's speech describe his dream of the United States as a nation in which his own children would not be judged by the color of their skin but "by the content of their character." Another key part of his speech spoke about the need for blacks and whites to work together, nonviolently, for integration:

> Let us not seek to satisfy our thirst for freedom by drinking from the cup of bitterness and hatred. We must forever conduct our struggle on the high plane of dignity and discipline. We must not allow our creative protest to degenerate into physical violence. Again and again we must rise to the majestic heights of meeting physical force with soul force.
>
> The marvelous new militancy which has engulfed the Negro community must not lead us to a

distrust of all white people, for many of our white brothers, as evidenced by their presence here today, have come to realize that their destiny is tied up with our destiny and they have come to realize that their freedom is inextricably bound to our freedom. This offense we share mounted to storm the battlements of injustice must be carried forth by a bi-racial army. We cannot walk alone.[22]

King had a dream, but for many, black and white, it was a dream that should have always been a reality.

Students and Freedom Riders Test Integration in the South

To succeed, the civil rights movement had to win the heart of the country. It was an African American movement, with black leadership and black volunteers working in demonstrations and voter registration, working throughout the country, but especially in the South, for freedom. To succeed, the civil rights movement also required thousands of white volunteers, willing and ready to integrate, willing to work for civil rights for their black brothers and sisters. It required the goodwill of American voters and the support of the federal government, from politicians to FBI agents to numerous rulings from the Supreme Court.

Freedom Riders Challenge Segregation

In the summer of 1961, young volunteers called Freedom Riders began to use nonviolent demonstrations to prick the conscience and raise the consciousness of many Americans. Both black and white, these volunteers tested bus desegregation in the South with a Freedom Ride Campaign. Organized by the Congress of Racial Equality (CORE) and members of the Student Nonviolent Coordinating Committee (SNCC), they toured the South in racially integrated buses and challenged the illegal "white only" waiting rooms in Greyhound bus terminals throughout the South.

The Freedom Riders were attacked and harassed at many points along their journey. In Anniston, Alabama, they were attacked by a stone-throwing mob and their bus tires were slashed. Carloads of whites chased the bus out of town. When it stopped six miles later to fix the tires, the bus was firebombed. Whites clubbed and beat the Freedom Riders when they ran from the smoke-filled bus. Fortunately,

an undercover state patrolman stopped the mob by firing his pistol in the air. The bus burned to the ground and twelve riders had to be treated for injuries and smoke inhalation.

The town of Anniston met the next wave of Freedom Riders, traveling on the Trailways bus line, with another mob attack. The riders survived, only to be ambushed in Birmingham, Alabama, where some were beaten unconscious. In both Anniston and Birmingham, local police did not try

Freedom Riders catch their breath outside their firebombed bus after having been beaten and clubbed by angry whites as the Freedom Riders tried to escape the smoke and the flames.

to prevent the attacks. The Freedom Riders, shaken and beaten, were still ready to continue the ride, but the bus drivers were afraid to drive them any farther south. They flew the rest of the way to New Orleans, Louisiana, but other students and older adults of both races flooded into Birmingham and continued the Freedom Rides. The Freedom Riders were determined to continue. Birmingham police arrested some and dropped them on a country road at the Alabama-Tennessee state line in the middle of the night. They simply found their way back to Birmingham and joined the Freedom Ride to Montgomery.

Montgomery segregationists met Freedom Riders on May 20 with a rioting mob who beat the students, journalists, and sympathetic whites and blacks for two hours. A federal official sent by President Kennedy to monitor the situation was beaten unconscious and left on the ground for twenty minutes. In spite of the violence, local police stayed clear, doing nothing to prevent or stop the mob attacks.

Kennedy had to send federal troops to restore the peace. Without federal intervention, southern segregationists generally felt free to ignore federal laws under the protection of local police. Although they had lost the Civil War,

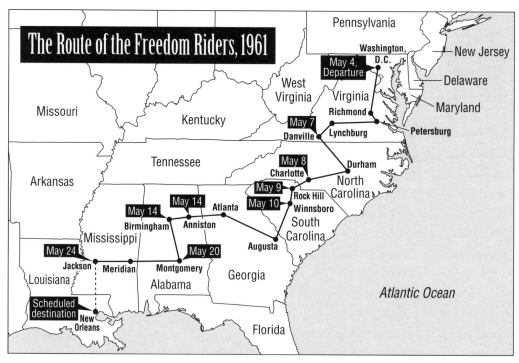

The Route of the Freedom Riders, 1961

when it came to matters of racial segregation many southern officials acted as if the South were a separate country, where they ruled like kings, and where African Americans still had to obey white "masters" as if they were slaves.

Voting Rights

Many southern laws reinforced blacks' second-class status. Since the Civil War, southerners had made literacy tests an especially effective tool to keep African Americans from voting and sharing political power. If necessary, they made blacks recite the entire U.S. Constitution from memory, and failed blacks for any "mispronunciation." Whites, on the other hand, could usually avoid the test altogether because a "grandfather clause" exempted anyone whose grandfather had voted before the Civil War. Since African American grandparents had been slaves without voting rights, blacks were always required to take the test. In addition to reading tests, the poll tax and property requirements placed a greater burden on poor African Americans than on wealthier white citizens who wanted to vote.

If they were able to pass the reading test, pay the tax, and prove property ownership, blacks still had to face the "white only" clause in primary elections. In a primary, voters choose which candidates may run for election.

Kept from voting in the primaries, blacks were rarely able to get their own candidates on the ballot.

Many civil rights leaders thought voting was the key that would unlock the handcuffs of racial segregation. They reasoned that if African Americans were able to vote, they could get political power in their own communities, in their states, and in their nation. Then they could start to make decisions for themselves that would help them do better in every aspect of their lives, from better school boards and education to better jobs, health care, and the right to freely enter public places.

Since they were a minority in the South, blacks needed the help of sympathetic white voters at the national level to support them. To achieve this, civil rights leaders tried to continue to make African Americans and their problems more visible in the national media.

To demonstrate how many black Mississippians wanted to vote but were not able to register, two New Yorkers from very different backgrounds came together to create a mock election in Mississippi. Robert Moses, an African American, held a master's degree in philosophy from Harvard and was a member of SNCC. He joined forces with Allard Lowenstein, a white Jew who was assistant dean of Stanford

University. Since it was difficult and dangerous for blacks to vote in the South in real elections, these men decided to run a mock election called the Freedom Vote of 1963. Some ninety thousand blacks "voted" in the pretend "Freedom" election in Mississippi, run alongside the real vote. This showed that blacks would vote, if allowed. The Freedom Vote also hinted that the "real" election was not legitimate. It could not represent all the voters of Mississippi, since so many potential voters were kept away from the polls by unfair reading tests, poll taxes, and intimidation.

Many local blacks were afraid to register, even in a mock election. Some asked Bob Moses if they could use false names on Freedom Vote registration rolls, to protect themselves and their families from being murdered as civil rights workers and "uppity" blacks had been in the past.

The next summer, Moses and Lowenstein worked to register blacks for legal voting. During a speech he called "Mississippi: A Foreign Country in Our Midst?," Lowenstein announced their summer project to an umbrella organization of civil rights groups called the Council of Federated Organizations (COFO) at their statewide convention. Freedom summer was designed not only to register more black voters, but, if need be, to show the country that African Americans in the South wanted to vote but faced great danger when they tried to do so.

Fear and Danger Stalk Civil Rights Workers

Segregationists had traditionally used fear to keep African Americans in their "place" in society, and the civil rights movement brought that tradition out in the open. King had been the target of bomb threats as early as 1956 when, in the midst of the Montgomery bus boycott, on January 30, a bomb was thrown on his front porch, putting his wife and infant daughter in jeopardy. The following January an unexploded bomb was discovered on his front porch. In September 1958 he was stabbed in the chest while autographing his new book in Harlem.

King survived that attack, but no civil rights leader was truly safe, especially in the South, where white segregationists often supported murder and violence against blacks. NAACP leader Medgar Evers was murdered just outside his own home in Jackson, Mississippi, on June 12, 1963. His murderer, Byron de la Beckwith, privately bragged about killing Evers, claiming "I believe in segregation like I believe in God."[23] His fingerprints were on the murder weapon, but he was twice

Voter Registration: A Firsthand Account

Fannie Lou Hamer was vice chairman of a delegation of voters registered by SNCC volunteers. They challenged the right of the segregationist delegation from their state to represent Mississippi at the Democratic National Convention. The following is a small part of her testimony about voter registration harassment in Mississippi taken from *"Takin' It to the Streets."* This testimony was covered in televised hearings before the Credentials Committee, on August 22, 1964, the Saturday before the convention began. Lyndon Johnson, trying to calm the convention members that were going to elect him as their presidential candidate, interrupted Hamer's testimony with a presidential announcement, and then sent his vice presidential candidate, Hubert Humphrey, to negotiate a settlement. He offered two seats as "delegates at large" to the challengers, but Ms. Hamer said: "We didn't come here for no two seats." She and her delegation returned to Mississippi, angry with the Democratic Party's lack of commitment to civil rights. The all-white segregationist delegates from Mississippi represented her state at the convention that year.

It was on the 31st of August 1962 that 18 of us traveled 26 miles to the county courthouse in Indianola to try to register to try to become first-class citizens.

We was met in Indianola by Mississippi men, Highway Patrolmens, and they only allowed two of us to take the literacy test at the time. After we had taken this test and started back to Ruleville, we was held up to the City Police and the State Highway Patrolmen and carried back to Indianola where the bus driver was charged that day with driving a bus the wrong color.

After we paid the fine among us, we continued on to Ruleville, and Reverend Jeff Sunnie carried me four miles in the rural area where I had worked as a timekeeper and sharecropper for 18 years. I was met there by my children, who told me the plantation owner was angry because I had gone down to try to register.

After they told me, my husband came, and said the plantation owner was raising Cain because I had tried to register, and before he quit talking the plantation owner came, and said, "Fannie Lou, do you know—did Pap tell you what I said?"

And I said, "Yes sir."

He said, "I mean that," he said, "If you don't go down and withdraw your registration, you will have to leave . . . you might have to go because we are not ready for that in Mississippi."

And I addressed him and told him and said "I didn't try to register for you. I tried to register for myself."

I had to leave that same night.

acquitted by an all-white jury. Beckwith was finally found guilty in a new trial over twenty years later. In the sixties, segregationists were fighting back, getting away with murder, and civil rights activists, both black and white, knew they faced real danger when they stood up for equal rights.

The movement was poorly protected because southern law enforcement often fought on the side of segregationists. In an example that received national media coverage, in one three-day confrontation, from May 3 through 5, 1963, Eugene ("Bull") O'Connor, the director of public safety of Birmingham, Alabama, ordered fire hoses and police dog attacks on marching protesters, many of whom were young adults and children.

Other southern officials resorted to outright murder: On June 23, 1964, three civil rights workers who had gone out to investigate a Mississippi church burning were reported missing in the *New York Times*. The Justice Department announced Attorney General Robert Kennedy's orders for a full federal kidnapping investigation under the 1936 Lindbergh law. The FBI sent agents to Neshoba County from New Orleans the next day.

Neshoba County's Sheriff Lawrence Rainey and deputy Cecil Price admitted that they had arrested the three civil rights workers for speeding and then held them for six hours. The officers told reporters they had released them safely. "If they're missing," said Rainey, "they just hid somewhere trying to get a lot of publicity out of it, I figure."[24]

Church Bombings

Since churches were often used as meeting halls for the civil rights movement, average parishioners were also at risk. In one of the saddest incidents of the sixties, four young girls were murdered when a bomb exploded in a Birmingham, Alabama, church just two weeks after King's inspiring March on Washington. According to *Pillar of Fire*, on Sunday, September 15, 1963, "A concussion of flying bricks and glass destroyed a bathroom inside the staircase wall, where four adolescent girls were preparing to lead the annual Youth Day worship service at eleven, wearing white for the special occasion. Seconds later, a dazed man emerged clutching a dress shoe from the foot of his eleven-year-old granddaughter, one of four mangled corpses in the rubble. His sobbing hysteria spread around the world before nightfall. The Communist oracle *Izvestia* of Moscow raised a common cry with the Vatican newspaper in Rome, which bemoaned a 'massacre of the innocents.'"

Federal Help for Civil Rights

President Johnson was determined to get the South to obey the laws, just like any other part of the country. In general, the Federal Bureau of Investigation had allowed Mississippi to follow its own laws and customs. Johnson knew the FBI usually bowed to director J. Edgar Hoover's strong prejudice against blacks, Jews, and others. Until then, Hoover had allowed

Mississippi to remain the only state without an FBI office. Johnson felt that as long as the FBI—under Hoover's direction—supported segregation, African Americans would not achieve their civil rights. Johnson pressured Hoover to send FBI agents to the state, warning him that he would tell the press that he had asked for additional men, and therefore, Hoover had better send them. In a phone conversation recorded in the White House, Johnson said:

> I called Edgar Hoover and told him to fill Mississippi—I can't say this publicly—but load it down with FBI men and put 'em in every place they anticipate they can as informers and put 'em in the Klan and infiltrate it and get 'em to join up—we can't advertise this. But get all the informers they need so we know what's going on and that we can protect these kids as best we can. . . . So he's shipped the FBI in there and he's got them joining up on everything and they're trying to get in a position where they can be helpful. When these kids didn't show, night before last, yesterday morning we sent a new bunch of FBI in to supplement 'em. . . . The FBI's got two big groups that've gone in at my request, although I don't want to

be appearing to be directing this thing and appear that I'm invading the state and taking the rights of the Governor or Mayor. Nevertheless, I've quietly shown plenty of firmness and put plenty of power. . . . We've asked 'em for a report as quickly as they can get it.[25]

Federal investigators made the difference. By that night, FBI agents had arrested three men carrying shotguns in Itta Bena, Mississippi. Saturday's edition of the *Times* called the FBI arrests "the first sign anywhere in Mississippi of effective action to uphold the upholders of the Constitution."[26]

News Media Promote Civil Rights

Television played a large role in this murder case, and in civil rights issues generally. The civil rights movement came of age in a decade of economic prosperity and increased media coverage. It is questionable whether the movement would have been as effective in an earlier, pretelevision time, when sit-ins and demonstrations would not have appeared so vividly across the country and the world.

Television set a new standard for immediate, live reporting of national news, and challenged the print media to report it more vividly. In covering civil rights, television demonstrated in living color that all was not perfect in the American Dream, and connected the country instantly, from one coast to the other. For the first time, people frequently saw pictures of Americans who were not white, not middle class, not equal, and not willing to tolerate that second-class status any longer.

As the search for the missing civil rights volunteers continued, Walter Cronkite told his CBS news audience that the whole country was watching Mississippi. This state, a symbol of the segregated South, was being brought under federal jurisdiction at last.

Federal Protection from Local Terror

But it was too late for the three civil rights workers. Their burned car was found in the Pearl River. Five days after they were declared missing, Bob Moses, announced "The kids are dead." FBI agents found their bodies on August 4, buried near Philadelphia, Mississippi. Sheriff Rainey and his deputy,

Supreme Court Justices Change Civil Rights

Thurgood Marshall argued for integration and won, for his nation, for his race, and personally. By 1967 the social climate of the United States—and the mood of voters—was so changed that with congressional approval, President Johnson was able to appoint Thurgood Marshall as the first African American justice of the Supreme Court. Ironically, Marshall's own arguments before the Supreme Court paved the way for integration in the United States in the midfifties, making his appointment possible. He served as a justice of the Supreme Court from 1967 to 1991.

Marshall graduated from Howard University in 1933 and went into private law practice in Baltimore. He joined the legal staff of the National Association for the Advancement of Colored People (NAACP) in 1936 and, as their chief counsel (1938–61) argued over thirty cases before the U.S. Supreme Court to successfully challenge segregation. His forceful arguments against the doctrine of "separate but equal" led to the landmark *Brown v. Board of Education* decision (1954), which provided the legal basis for integration in schools and public places. On the Supreme Court, Marshall consistently supported the rights of those discriminated against on the basis of race or gender. He opposed the death penalty, upheld the rights of criminal defendants, and supported affirmative action to give blacks and women an equal footing with white men in the workplace.

Marshall's opinions were often supported by another Supreme Court justice, William J. Brennan. For example, Brennan applied the *Brown* ruling to a northern school district for the first time in the case of *Keyes v. School District No. 1 of Denver* in 1973.

Remembering those who died for integration, Dr. King holds a picture of the three civil rights workers killed in Mississippi.

hear King speak. Protected by federal troops, they were safely joined by over twenty-five thousand more marchers.

But federal troops could not prevent violence entirely. The wife of a Detroit Teamsters Union official, Mrs. Viola Luizzo, was shot and killed when she attempted to drive a carload of those same marchers back to Selma. Similarly, on March 9, 1965, James Reeb, a Unitarian minister, was beaten to death in Selma by four white segregationists. That same month, sheriff's deputies and police on horseback beat black and white demonstrators in Montgomery.

Cecil Price, were thought to be behind the murders.

In spite of the violence, or perhaps because of it, support for segregation was weakening, at least at the national level. Now when local sheriffs endangered lives instead of protecting the right to protest, federal troops stepped in to protect the rights of integration demonstrators. On March 21–25, 1965, over three thousand protesters marched from Selma to Montgomery to

Washington Supports Civil Rights Legislation

Congress had opened the decade by passing the landmark Voting Rights Act on April 21, 1960. This gave all citizens, whatever their race or religion, the right to vote without having to pay a poll tax or pass an unfair reading test. Now Congress responded to Johnson's leadership, the power of King's message, the nonviolent protests of civil rights workers and leaders throughout the country, and the growing national demand for justice. As Johnson pointed out in his first address to a joint session of Congress after Kennedy's assassination, "We have talked long enough in this country about equal civil rights. We have talked for a hundred years or more."[27] It was time for action.

On June 29, 1964, senators and congressmen finally passed the civil rights bill. On Thursday, July 2, President Johnson signed it into law in the presence of Martin Luther King, Robert Kennedy, Hubert Humphrey, and over one hundred others who had worked to pass it. This historic bill banned the Jim Crow laws of the South and segregated practices throughout the country. It prohibited discrimination in voting, jobs, and public accommodations. The Supreme Court had ruled that separate facilities were inherently unequal. Now federal law made separate facilities a federal crime.

On August 6, 1965, Johnson signed the Voting Rights Act of 1965, a stronger version of the 1960 Voting Rights Act. Following the 1965 bill, the number of blacks registered to vote increased from 29 to 52 percent. By 1968, it would reach 3 million, or 60 percent, the same percentage as white voters. With civil rights and the right to vote protected at the federal level, the entire nation was now legally required to respect the rights of all its citizens equally, without regard to race, religion, or gender.

Assassination Strikes Again

These legal gains came at great personal cost, especially for those leading the movement. Tragically, on April 4, 1968, Martin Luther King was assassinated in Memphis, Tennessee, allegedly shot by an escaped convict named James Earl Ray while the Reverend Jesse Jackson and others stood by, unable to help him.

President Johnson declared Sunday, April 7, 1968, a day of national mourning. Overcome with anger and despair, many African Americans took to the streets in riots that exploded in 125 cities. More than fifty thousand National Guard and federal troops were called up to restore order, but not before forty-six people, all but five of them black, died.

This was not the first time riots had exploded in black communities across the country. The contrast between the dream of freedom and the nightmare of daily life had fueled the Watts riot in Los Angeles in 1965, which killed thirty-four people and caused over $200 million in property damage. The next three summers saw riots in over 150 cities. Dozens of people were killed and hundreds of millions of dollars' worth of property were destroyed in these outbursts of anger and frustration. Riots proved self-defeating, especially for black communities whose own neighborhoods were destroyed. While riots frightened and angered many, they also emphasized the urgency of improving daily life for African Americans.

Assassinations Increase Desperation

Assassinations helped fuel the desperation that led to many of these riots. More leaders were assassinated in the United States in the five years between 1963 and 1968 than in any previous decade. All of them were leaders of liberal or radical left movements, from John Kennedy, Robert Kennedy, and Martin Luther King to Malcolm X. These men, bringing hope to so many in life, brought despair in the wake of their deaths. Many of their supporters became more desperate and more open to radical solutions as a result of their murders.

Black Radicals Gain Followers

For those disappointed in American life, the Black Muslims offered dignity, self-respect, religion, and separatism as an alternative to integration. Founded in Detroit by Wali

King's Alleged Assassins

James Earl Ray was arrested in England several weeks after the murder of Martin Luther King and confessed, but then recanted his confession. King had received many death threats over the years, and his father and others charged that there had been a conspiracy to kill him, possibly involving members of the U.S. government and perhaps the Federal Bureau of Investigation. The FBI had been informed of death threats against King, but their protection of him was questionable.

The FBI, under J. Edgar Hoover's direction, had secretly wiretapped and spied on him, with approval of first President Kennedy and then Johnson. FBI director Hoover viewed King as a secret "communist" and therefore a threat to the country. As Harris Wofford, President Kennedy's appointee on civil rights, recounts in *Of Kennedy and Kings*, "On the memorial march in Memphis and during the long day in Atlanta, for the first time I heard associates of King express their suspicions that somehow J. Edgar Hoover was directly involved in King's death. Since then, as evidence of Hoover's and the FBI's extraordinary campaign against King has come to light, those suspicions have grown. . . . In 1979 further evidence of Hoover's obsession with King and his determination to rid the country of his influence was presented in the hearings of the House Select Committee on Assassinations. 'We were operating an intensive vendetta against Dr. King in an effort to destroy him,' testified Atlanta FBI agent Murtagh.'"

Farad, Black Muslims coupled strict codes of personal behavior and religion with ideas of separating from white America. Farad mysteriously disappeared in 1934, and was succeeded by Elijah Muhammad, who moved the organization to Chicago.

Elijah Muhammad reached out especially to blacks who were poor and imprisoned, calling white men devils for the oppression and racism they had practiced. He preached that blacks were God's chosen people. His sect, numbering about eight thousand, gained thousands of new followers in the sixties, especially in response to the preaching of one of his most articulate ministers, Malcolm X.

In 1963, Malcolm X broke with Elijah Muhammad and founded the Organization of Afro-Americans, which advocated not separatism but interracial civil war. Malcolm X was assassinated in February, 1965, possibly by Elijah Muhammad's followers.

Black Panthers

Among the strongest of the black separatist movements was the Black Panthers, founded in California in 1966 by Huey Newton and Bobby Seale. Active in Chicago and other large cities, they attempted to organize black neighborhoods and

Black Muslims Split

The world champion prizefighter Cassius Clay renamed himself Muhammad Ali to follow the Black Muslim policy that rejected white slave names. He was jailed when he refused to go into "the white man's army" for the war in Vietnam. He eventually broke with Malcolm X, preferring to stay with Elijah Muhammad.

This and other splits in the Muslim organization led to much debate and some regret among Black Muslims. In *Muhammad Ali: His Life and Times,* for which he was interviewed, Ali later said, "It was a pity and a disgrace he died like that, because what Malcolm saw was right, and after he left us, we went his way anyway. Color didn't make a man a devil. It's the heart, soul, and mind that counts."

Muhammad Ali won his first world heavyweight title in 1964.

protect African American communities from police harassment by promoting self-policing and self-determination. The Panthers called on blacks to arm themselves and liberate blacks through violent revolution.

This made them a threat to the U.S. government. The Panthers, gaining strength in the inner cities, were targeted by the FBI under President Nixon. By 1969, twenty-eight Panthers had been killed by police, and many more arrested.

Civil Rights Connects with Other Movements

With Gandhi-inspired methods of nonviolence, the civil rights movement shaped the strategies and tactics of many other movements for equality. The civil rights movement inspired and often overlapped other causes, including women's liberation and the causes of other minorities such as Chicano migrant workers, Hispanics, American Indians, and the antiwar movement.

The antiwar movement especially linked itself to civil rights and the plight of African Americans. Civil rights protests were supported by a

Bobby Seale (left) and Huey Newton (holding gun) rejected nonviolence and called for armed revolution.

vast number of the baby boom generation, and especially white college students, who saw connections between racism, the war economy, and the war in Vietnam. By the end of the sixties, these issues were often connected into larger protests against institutional racism and support for the military. For example, in 1968, students at Columbia University protested both the university's racism (as demonstrated in the way it interacted with the black neighborhoods surrounding the college campus) and its links to the military, from military research in the math department to Dow Chemical recruitment among chemistry students. Over 700 students were arrested and 148 injured before 1,000 police officers were able to end the week-long, highly publicized demonstration.

Reclaiming an African Heritage

In the process of pursuing equal civil rights, African Americans also made a deeper exploration and affirmation of their own heritage and culture. They had been called names and ridiculed by whites for generations. Now people who had been called Colored and Negro were renaming themselves Black, pure and simple, taking the darkest skin color of their race and claiming it with pride. Many began to study their African roots and the unique cultural contributions blacks have made to the United States and the world. African hairstyles, from corn rows to Afros, became popular as many African Americans stopped straightening their hair and "dressing white," and began instead to add dashikis and other African clothes to their wardrobe. Black students demanded that universities add black studies to the college curriculum. Across the country, many blacks and whites studied the music, dance, art, poetry, and literature of Africans and African Americans with renewed interest and appreciation.

Lasting Changes

The decade began with African Americans working to put their court-won equal rights into practice across the country. It ended with increased political strength for black Americans, and a deeper exploration and affirmation of African American heritage and culture. Black rage at unfair economic, social, and political practices served to add teeth to the civil rights movement, although it usually hurt black communities when it exploded into riots.

The sixties saw a critical change in attitudes about racial segregation. When the decade began, people had debated whether or not the races should be segregated. This dialogue increased as black separatists proposed self-determination and violent revolution. By the end of the decade, the question most Americans faced, given the alternatives, was no longer *if* segregation should exist, but rather *how* it should be ended.

Chapter Five

Young men faced jail when they said no to their country's war.

Countercultures Provide Alternatives

Countercultures, or groups of people who seek alternatives to the accepted ways of doing things, thrived in the sixties as people began to explore personal and political change. The strongest force behind the formation of countercultures came from the baby boom generation as they actively sought alternatives to their parents' values and goals. This generation domi-

nated the population of the United States in sheer numbers, making them a powerful agent for change.

The countercultures of the sixties spanned a variety of interests and approaches, but most were recognized by the clothes and attitudes that the press labeled "hippies." Rejecting the conformist, clean-cut look of their parents, many baby boomers, male and female, began to grow long hair, wear colorful beads, unusual earrings, and ragged jeans and put flowers in their hair. This was not a look that would get young people jobs on Wall Street. That was the point. Although what they wore seemed outrageous to the conformist society they were rebelling against, few of their fashion choices would cause alarm today.

Haircuts: The First Youth Rebellion

It was a decade when men still wore dress hats to baseball games and women wore white gloves to church. Even simple changes in the length of boys' hair prompted intense objections from adults. For example, the morning after the rock group the Beatles made their American debut on the Ed Sullivan show on February 9, 1964, many boys combed their one-inch long hair forward to copy what was called the Beatles' "mop," instead of combing it back. Some were suspended from school for the day, and told to get a haircut.

Most high schools had strict dress codes that did not allow girls to wear pants, even on the coldest days of a northern winter. Knee-length dresses and stockings were the norm. Once students arrived at colleges and universities with more relaxed dress codes, most wore jeans whenever they could. Their parents thought they looked sloppy; most baby boomer students simply felt freer than they ever had in their lives.

Marijuana Is Passed to a New Generation

Hippies were strongly influenced by the beatniks of the Beat generation, a small group of American artists and writers who rejected the mainstream values of the fifties. Beats loved progressive jazz and bebop music, explored free artistic expression and Eastern mysticism, and often experimented with mescaline, marijuana, and other drugs.

Baby boomers smoked marijuana and found that it changed their attitudes in significant ways. Most liked the change, and many became hippies under its influence. An ancient, intoxicating weed, marijuana produces increased sensitivity to colors, music, and other stimuli. It distorts a person's sense of time and promotes introspection and passivity when smoked or ingested. Widely grown in South America and grown as a source of rope fiber in the United States since colonial times, it is thought to have been first introduced into the United States as an intoxicant in the early twentieth century by Mexican laborers and Latin American seamen.

Office workers walk past hippies smoking marijuana in Haight-Ashbury in 1967.

The U.S. government launched a strong campaign against marijuana use in the thirties, claiming that it is highly addictive and leads to abuse of hard drugs. This has been largely disproved, but marijuana does limit a user's ability to think clearly, use good judgment, and perform well while under its influence. It has mild physical side effects, including increased appetite, dry mouth, slowed physical responses, impaired judgment, and distorted perception that make it dangerous to use, especially when driving.

Marijuana is not medically in the same class as physically addictive drugs, but has been sold on the streets by organized crime syndicates for decades, often as a way of encouraging harder drug use by association. It remains against the law to sell marijuana, although it is approved in some instances for medical treatment of cancer patients to relieve nausea and improve appetite.

Although strictly illegal, marijuana was almost as available as tobacco in the sixties from a variety of sources, both imported and homegrown. Students discovered marijuana at college, civil rights activists found it in African American communities, and musicians found it widely used in their business world. Vietnam soldiers, if they had not discovered it at home, found extremely potent marijuana available in Vietnam.

The hippie counterculture often claimed that marijuana threatened the dominant cultural values of achievement and productivity. They pointed out that their parents' drug of choice, tobacco, contains highly addictive nicotine, which promotes improved concentration and heightened activity. In contrast, marijuana promotes a more passive, sensual enjoyment of the present moment. Marijuana use in the sixties became both a recreational drug and a way to oppose the dominant culture's goals and values.

LSD and Timothy Leary Promoted by *Life* Magazine

Another, more powerful drug also became associated with the sixties. While marijuana creates a dreamy state, other drugs induce semipsychotic states, sometimes pleasurable, often frightening. The most potent of these is lysergic acid diethylamide, or LSD. Five thousand times more potent than mesca-

LSD Was Legal in the Sixties

When LSD was outlawed in California on October 6, 1966, Haight-Ashbury hippies and political activists decided to protest. As Allen Cohen remembers in Gene Anthony's *Summer of Love,* hippies typically tried to live out their ideals, and say no their way: "Without confrontation. We wanted to create a celebration of innocence. We were not guilty of using illegal substances. We were celebrating transcendental consciousness. The beauty of the universe. The beauty of being."

They requested a permit from the city and the rally was a joyful success by hippie terms: everyone had a good time. LSD remained illegal, however, and drug use, especially of addictive heroin or cocaine, ruined many young lives. Drug pushers often added cheaper, but more dangerous, substances to LSD, such as strychnine, a poison. It became increasingly difficult to get pure LSD, and even pure LSD often produced negative side effects, such as repeated hallucinations when "off" the drug.

line, its effects include hallucinations that last from six to fourteen hours. One of the reasons drug use became widely popular in the sixties was, oddly enough, through mainstream *Life* magazine's coverage of LSD and the work of Dr. Timothy Leary.

At Harvard University, Drs. Timothy Leary and Richard Alpert legally experimented with LSD. Leary and

Alpert's early work and enthusiasm for their own "expanded consciousness" (as a result of using LSD themselves) was covered with fascination in *Life* magazine. Leary's name soon became a household word. He began to recommend that people "turn on, tune in, and drop out" of society. By this he meant people should "turn on" their inner vision with LSD, "tune in" to the cosmic vibrations of universal consciousness they seemed to contact while on the drug, and "drop out" of

Timothy Leary "tunes out" mainstream attitudes while living on his farm in Millbrook, New York, in 1967.

the competitive rat race of capitalist society. Some thought Leary had used a little too much LSD himself to be an impartial scientist regarding the drug.

Meditation as an Alternative to Drugs

Leary's partner Richard Alpert decided that the problem with LSD is that a person always comes down from a drug-induced high. Seeking an alternative, he found a guru of the Hindu religion in the Himalayas. There he learned to meditate to get a "natural" high that would not hurt body and mind the way drugs can. He adopted the spiritual name Ram Dass, wrote *Be Here Now* and other widely read books on meditation, founded a hospice organization to help people in the process of dying, and lectured for the next thirty years throughout the United States and the world. He encouraged a trend toward spiritual seeking that was yet another alternative to mainstream society, political solutions, or retreat from society through drugs or communes.

Interest in Eastern religions and culture increased throughout the sixties. Maharishi Mahesh Yogi brought the techniques of transcendental meditation, or TM, to the United States. The Beatles followed him to India in 1967 and announced they were going to give up drugs and follow his teachings. He immediately became popular throughout the Western world, and posters of him became a familiar sight. TM centers sprang up throughout the country, as did religious retreat communities for other meditation techniques and religions.

Ancient Drugs Lead to Modern Use and Abuse

Peyote and other "natural" hallucinogens from the American Indian and other traditions were tried by many baby boomers for both vision quests and as party drugs. Internationally known writer Aldous Huxley had popularized the use of mescaline with his 1954 essay "The Doors of Perception." Kiowa and Navajo Indians had used the mescaline-containing peyote cactus for generations in religious rituals to induce spiritual visions. Beginning in the 1950s, mescaline became available in crystal form, and from then on was typically ingested in capsules.

There Goes the Neighborhood: Hippies Take Over

Hippie communities flourished in cities throughout the United States, especially near universities with student movement and antiwar activities. Media coverage of the phenomenon at-

Hippies explore music and conversation in Haight-Ashbury in 1967.

tracted high school students, who began to join this trend on weekends, summer vacations, or long-term. The Haight-Ashbury district of San Francisco, with its warm climate and liberal atmosphere, became a mecca for hippies of all ages who sought to live outside of the American mainstream. The area was especially attractive to high school dropouts and runaways. According to writer Gene Anthony, "The kids kept coming. There were more of them every day. They arrived in cars and vans and on motorcycles and down at the Seventh Street Greyhound Bus terminal."[28]

One way to drop out of the system was to live as cheaply as possible. To this end, many hitchhiked clear across the country rather than pay for plane tickets or even gas. With a bedroll and a backpack, hippies often "crashed" with friends or slept in national and public parks, and adopted a semi-nomadic lifestyle.

Ideally, they shared what they had with one another. For example, a hand-bill distributed anonymously on Haight Street announced:

FREE BARTER
ON FREE (HAIGHT) STREET SUNDAY

WATCH FOR SIGNS
BRING YOUR STUFF
CLOTHES AND FABRICS
FOOD
KIDS' TOYS
FREE NEWS
ETC.

BRING DOWN WHAT YOU DON'T NEED
AND TAKE AWAY WHAT YOU WANT
HAIGHT STREET WILL BE
FREE STREET SUNDAY.
CELEBRATE THE STREET.
CELEBRATE THE DAY.

CELEBRATE.[29]

Hippies volunteered to support one another, providing many community services, from health care to coopera-tive grocery stores, for free or at cost. A free clinic in Haight-Ashbury was open twenty-four hours a day and offered a Calm Center to support people who were having "bad trips" on acid and other drugs.

Political groups such as the Diggers in San Francisco tried to create a politi-cal movement out of the communal lifestyle that was sprouting in hippie communities. The Diggers wrote a blueprint for a new society called *The Digger Papers*, in which they proposed dropping out of the competitive "war economy" and dominant culture by providing a free exchange of services. This would include a free city switch-board/information center, free food storage and distribution center, garage and mechanics, legal assistance, med-ical clinics, and even free housing, work space, and a "free city" bank and treasury. While some of these projects worked well for a time, drug use and obtaining drugs became the main activ-ity of many in the Haight. This trend destroyed the community from within long before it could achieve any lofty political ideals.

The New Left:
Counterculture Politics

There were hippies who focused on marijuana and other drugs, but others were more influenced by politics and the need to affirm peaceful, nonviolent rejection of what they saw as the war economy and its values. They were part of a trend that went beyond the borders of the United States. Baby boomers trav-eled more than their parents had, and found people of their generation in every country of the world who shared their questions and concerns. The counterculture in the United States found its counterparts in a student movement and hippie phenomenon that was worldwide. As the Beat generation writer William Burroughs wrote in his novel *Naked Lunch*, "The youth rebellion is a worldwide phenomenon that had not been seen in history. I do not believe they will calm down and be ad execs at thirty as the Establishment would like us to believe."[30]

The New Left emerged from the ashes of old socialists, labor unionists, communists, garden-variety liberals, and reaction to years of virulent McCarthy anticommunism, and took hold of the student movement. The issues of the war in Vietnam, civil rights, and the War on Poverty fueled the movement and provided unlimited occasions for protest and political activity. Protests mushroomed in number, size, and issues, and often transformed their participants, as this Columbia University student describes:

> My world had been very staid, very traditional, very frightened, very middle-class and respectable. And here I was doing these things that six months before I would have thought were just horrible. But I was in the midst of an enormous

tide of people. There was so much constant collective reaffirmation of it. The ecstasy was stepping out of time, out of traditional personal time. The usual rules of the game in capitalist society had been set aside. It was phenomenally liberating. . . . At the same time, it was a political struggle. It wasn't just Columbia. There *was* a . . . war going on in Vietnam, and the civil rights movement. These were profound forces that transcend that moment. 1968 just cracked the universe open for me. And the fact of getting involved meant that never again was I going to look at something outside with the kind of reflex condemnation or fear. Yes, it was the making of me—or the unmaking.[31]

Minority Cultures Join Forces with the Counterculture

While middle-class youth joined antiwar student movements and took on hippie attitudes, many members of minority groups such as African Americans, American Indians, and Hispanics began to assert their cultural identities. They insisted that their differences from the mainstream culture deserved respect and should be recognized in public life.

Most Americans can trace their families back to immigrants from one

Mexican American Farmworkers Adopt Nonviolence

Cesar Chavez went on a fast in 1968 to bring national attention to the plight of Mexican American migrant farmworkers, and to rededicate their struggle to the tactic of nonviolence. Robert Kennedy, worried for Chavez's health, convinced him to end his fast, and then spoke to his supporters. The speech is excerpted in *RFK Collected Speeches:*

Two years ago your union had not yet won a major victory. Now, elections have been held on ranch after ranch and the workers have spoken. They have spoken, and they have said, "We want a union. . . . The world must know, from this time forward, that the migrant farm worker, the Mexican-American, is coming into his own rights. You are winning a special kind of citizenship: no one is doing it for you—you are winning it for yourselves—and therefore no one can ever take it away.

And when your children and grandchildren take their place in America—going to high school, and college, and taking good jobs at good pay—when you look at

Labor organizer Cesar Chavez waves to the crowd at the California state capitol in Sacramento in 1966.

them, you will say, "I did this. I was there, at the point of difficulty and danger." And though you may be old and bent from many years of labor, no man will stand taller than you when you say, "I marched with Cesar."

country or another. In the past, immigrants usually tried to adopt the culture of the majority in the United States, who were white, Protestant, and middle class. As the civil rights movement began to highlight people who were not white or middle class, but who nonetheless had dignity and a vibrant culture of their own, the idea of what American culture looked and sounded like began to expand to include the wide variety of cultures actually present in the country. The spirit of equal rights was contagious and empowering. Other minorities began to challenge their own working and living conditions. The spirit of change, which many called revolution, seemed to fill the air.

Mexican Americans Affirm Their Culture and Rights

Mexican Americans began to call themselves Chicanos, affirming their own identity. Cesar Chavez formed the National Farm Workers Association (NFWA) in the early sixties to help improve working conditions for Chicano migrant workers. They were supported by the powerful national labor union, the AFL-CIO. When the NFWA staged a grape picker work stoppage in California in 1966, they began the largest strike by farmworkers in California history. Public support was strong across the nation, as people from all walks of life felt compassion for this group of hard-working, mistreated poor.

American Indians Fight for Treaty Rights, and Respect

American Indians, although less vocal in the streets, began to fight for their land rights in courts and insisted that the federal government honor their treaties and give back some of their land. They organized both on and off reservations to try to achieve social reform and improve their "most impoverished minority" status.

One of the most well known organizations for Indian rights was the confrontational American Indian Movement (AIM), founded by Dennis Banks and Clyde Bellancourt in 1968. In 1969, eighty-nine members of AIM reclaimed the island of Alcatraz, including the former prison, in San Francisco Bay. They demanded both the island's return to Indian control and money to found a center for Indian culture. They did not achieve their demands, but held the island until 1971.

Women and Other Minorities

Although they made up more than 50 percent of the population, women were often referred to as "women and other minorities" by those discussing social change and the women's movement. Since they lived longer than men, women were actually a majority in the United States in terms of numbers. But in terms of their power vis-à-vis white men, they were often invisible and as powerless as any minority.

Two things began to change women's status in the sixties: a book by

Reclaiming their rights and protesting broken treaties, Sioux Indians demonstrate on Alcatraz on March 9, 1964.

and changed attitudes toward sex. By preventing pregnancy, it changed women's risks and roles in the family and society. It made sex seem risk free, at least for pregnancy. Sexually transmitted diseases, predictably, increased. Remnants of Victorian and puritanical mores were challenged as some women joined the cry of the peace movement: "Make love, not war."

The pill had other, very concrete effects on society. It helped end the baby boom, since, for the first time in the history of humanity, women could choose to not have more children. It also allowed more women to feel free to enter the workforce full-time. Then abortion, long a dangerous, back-alley procedure, became legal. In 1967, Governor John Love of Colorado signed a bill that legalized abortion for victims of rape or incest or, significantly, for women who might be damaged emotionally by giving birth. This provided a legal option for women facing an unwanted pregnancy. Abortion was also legal if the unborn child was deformed. Many citizens objected to abortion on religious grounds, but others argued, "If you don't believe in abortion, don't have one." The issue of

Betty Friedan called *The Feminine Mystique*, which changed their minds, and a scientific breakthrough so important it was simply called the pill, which changed their reproductive choices.

The contraceptive pill gave women control over their own lives by allowing them to gain control over childbearing. First introduced in 1954 and widely available by 1960, the pill revolutionized women's childbearing years

The little pill that changed women's lives, giving them reliable control over their reproductive cycle for the first time.

as a writer, and other women tell me it changed theirs. I have had to take the responsibility for the revolution my words helped start."[32]

This change in attitudes about themselves was the most powerful, revolutionary aspect of the women's movement. Many women, for the first time, saw themselves as completely equal to men, and they began to insist that men treat them as equals in the workplace and at home.

Women's Liberation Supports Other Causes

Most women involved in the women's liberation movement were also against the war in Vietnam and active in supporting civil rights for blacks and other minorities. In the process of working for these causes, many women found that they were treated as second-class citizens within the movements they were trying to support. Women were expected to make coffee and take minutes of meetings, no matter how much experience they had in civil rights or antiwar activities.

choice, begun in the sixties, continued to be controversial for the rest of the century.

One Book Starts a Revolution

In 1963, Betty Friedan published the best-selling *The Feminine Mystique,* in which she questioned the limited roles that women were asked to play in society and challenged women to push beyond these false limits.

As Friedan later wrote, "I did not set out consciously to start a revolution when I wrote *The Feminine Mystique*, but it changed my life, as a woman and

Inspired by the ideas and tactics of the African American fight for civil rights, women began to change their attitudes about their role in society.

Women had been the last Americans to be given the vote, in 1928. Now they began to think that voting, education, and even money was not enough. They needed to see themselves differently; as strong, independent, and important in their own right, not just important when they served their families as wives, sisters, and mothers. Many women, kept at home by their responsibilities and provided for by their husbands, had money and education but no power, no independence or freedom to determine their own lives.

Fighting Against Stereotypes and Protesting War

Initially followers rather than leaders, women began to want a stronger role in the civil rights and antiwar movements. They were no longer content to simply play the role of secretary to the antiwar and civil rights movements. On March 26, 1969, women stood on their own against the war, organizing the Women Strike for Peace demonstration in Washington, D.C.

Others became active speakers, leading movements and running for elective office. Shirley Chisholm started as a state representative, then became the first black congresswoman in 1968. She and Marxist political activist Angela Davis and others explored the double prejudice they faced as black women. Women of every color and economic background joined the national conversation about racism, equal rights, feminism, and the war in Vietnam.

The Right to Be Different, Equal, and Free

Countercultures in the sixties affirmed the right to be different from the mainstream and they countered or resisted actions they felt were wrong, such as the Vietnam War, racism, and economic exploitation. In the process of challenging mainstream society, many countercultures explored alternatives that led them to a clearer understanding of themselves and the dominant culture they resisted. They also caused mainstream America to take stock of itself. Many Americans examined their beliefs, their dress codes, their customs and values. Some were well satisfied with the status quo; others found parts, or all, of their lives that they wished to change.

By the end of the sixties, American culture had been seriously challenged on every level, from the most trivial issues of hairstyle to matters of life, death, and what it means to be an American citizen. In the process, friendships, families, communities, and the country itself was in many ways shaken to the core.

Chapter Six

Hippies share a car and flash the peace sign at the Woodstock music festival.

Arts and Entertainment Reflect the Counterculture

Politics, social change, and even psychedelic drugs altered people's awareness in the sixties. Artists affected by these trends began to explore new ways to expand their artistic expression, creating new art movements in the process. While television and most movies continued to express mainstream cultural values throughout the decade, theater, visual arts, fashion, literature, and especially music began to reflect the youth counterculture and its need to explore alternatives.

In the visual arts, artists such as Andy Warhol, Peter Max, and Roy Lichtenstein combined old and new techniques, and mixed the images of popular culture and everyday objects. Lichtenstein began as an abstract expressionist painter but became famous for his enlarged panels from comic strips. One of the best-known and most challenging artists of the sixties, Andy Warhol also glorified comic strips, among other things. He enlarged and printed multiple images of them, as he did with his paintings and silk screen reproductions of everyday images, such as Campbell's soup cans and the faces of celebrities, including his famous series of Marilyn Monroe.

Another well-known artist of the time, Peter Max, combined undulating graphic designs, bright vibrating colors, and art nouveau style with floral and celestial images to create pieces that looked "psychedelic," or similar to fanciful visions people often saw while on LSD. His work was polished and commercial enough to make a fortune on posters, fabrics, accessories, and advertisements.

Other artists, such as Victor Vasarely, Richard Anusziewicz, and Bridget Riley created drawings and paintings that appeared to move. They helped develop Op art, so-called because it worked with color and patterns to create illusions of pulsation, movement, and other tricks to fool the eye. Op art developed in the United States and Europe in the 1960s out of the abstract expressionist movement. It was given a large exhibition at the Museum of Modern Art in New York in 1965.

Told to look at soup cans and comics as if they were Rembrandts and Renoirs, and at optical illusions that truly fooled their perception, the general public was at times amused and intrigued. More often than not, the older generation was baffled by these new artistic trends.

Fashion Expresses a New Nonconformity

In this time of social change, fashion began to reflect a need to break with tradition and search for individuality. There were still fashion rules—dresses were shorter, inching up toward the first "mini" skirts, and every woman went along with this, at least as far as above the knee. Men let their hair grow longer, experimenting with sideburns and even "mutton chops," or sideburns that broadened onto the cheek. Some pierced one ear. Even the most conservative men began wearing a softer, less military haircut. Businessmen tried to loosen up, sporting "leisure suits" in their off hours, usually made of a particularly uncomfortable polyester.

Words such as "mod" and "fab" described such clothes as vinyl miniskirts and the experimental "disposable" dresses made of paper. The fashion conscious had fun exploring space-age fabrics and designs. Psychedelic designs on fabric included clothing that changed color under black lights. Bright colors and bold patterns drew from both Op art and LSD/marijuana "psychedelic" trends.

The Eastern influence that had seeped into philosophy, nonviolent sit-ins, and the arts found its way into clothing, as well. Nehru jackets for men, which sported a small stand-up collar in place of western lapels, patterned after the lightweight jackets of India's premier, Jawaharlal Nehru, became popular. The Far East also introduced gauzy, embroidered blouses for women. Some feminists stopped wearing bras, and many hippies wore sandals most of the time. It was a time to experiment with possibilities, head to toe. For hippies, it was a time to simplify: cotton jeans and a T-shirt tie-dyed in the kitchen sink became a unisex uniform for many.

Performance Art and "Happenings"

Eastern philosophy had gradually entered into the artistic consciousness of the United States with subtle ideas about valuing the act of being as much as Western culture had always valued doing. As the political sit-in became a standard act of civil resistance, be-ins promoted a form of musical-political experience that honored simple existence. In a time when war was killing thousands, the right to be seemed important.

"Happenings" expanded the forms of artistic expression by combining visual art, performance, and audience participation. Artists such as Claes Oldenburg, Allan Kaprow, and Lucas

Artist Claes Oldenburg shows off the giant ice cream cone he created in his Greenwich Village studio.

Samaras began "Happenings" in the early 1960s, creating unpredictable, one-of-a-kind artistic events. For example, Oldenburg created *The Store* (1962), a false grocery through which his audience could roam freely, and other food-centered plaster and "soft sculpture" expressions made of stuffed cloth, including *The Giant Hamburger* (1963) and *Soft Fur Good Humors,* which showed both the ingenious and grotesque sides of fast food. Over time, happenings became events that focused more on music interwoven with light shows than on visual art or audience interactions with performers.

A well-known performance artist was Yoko Ono, who later married and collaborated with Beatle John Lennon. An artist with groundbreaking ideas, in 1966 Yoko Ono staged a happening in which the audience was asked to cut away pieces of her clothing for an hour as she knelt silently. In 1967, she staged her first art exhibit in London, which consisted of designs for half-finished furniture. Her book of poems, *Grapefruit*, described many directions for personal happenings intended to bring readers a sense of connection with the world, living things, and their own imagination. Sample recipes included:

A trailblazing performance artist, poet, and musician, Yoko Ono brought unique contributions to the arts and strongly influenced Beatle John Lennon.

LIGHT PIECE
Carry an empty bag.
Go to the top of the hill.
Pour all the light you can in it.
Go home when it is dark.
Hang the bag in the middle of your room in place of a light bulb.

PEA PIECE
Carry a bag of peas.
Leave a pea wherever you go.

MASK PIECE
Wear a blank mask.
Ask people to put in wrinkles, dimples
eyes, mouth, etc., as you go.[33]

Theater

Politics and the desire to inform the public about current issues inspired artists and performers to try new ways to express their views. Experimental theater groups sprang up from coast to coast, educating the public through a more entertaining method than by pamphlets or speeches. An especially effective group was El Teatro Campesino, which dramatized the lives and plight of migrant farmworkers with skits and music.

Many musicians and artists collaborated to redefine art and merge it into a more action-oriented form. Out of this effort, experimental performances arose. The Living Theater, a group of actors who lived together, experimented with improvisation in ways that influenced theater around the world.

One of the best-known groups still performing today is the San Francisco Mime Troupe, begun in 1959 and directed by R. G. Davis as guerrilla or street theater. The term "guerrilla" comes from guerrilla warfare, where fighters use surprise or improvisational tactics to harass the enemy. Similarly, guerrilla theater often surprises pedestrians on streets and in parks with unannounced performances.

Performing both in its own theater and in public places, the San Francisco Mime Troupe helped raise money for political action groups such as SNCC, CORE, and antiwar organizations. Today, it continues to tie the theme of its skits and plays to current political issues and weaves political satire into its lines. As with most street productions, its outdoor performances are free of charge, relying on passing the hat for donations toward costs and causes.

One of the most successful underground theater productions in the sixties was *MacBird!* by Barbara Garson. Garson parodied Shakespeare's *Macbeth* by portraying Lyndon and Lady Bird Johnson as Macbeth and Lady Macbeth, renamed MacBird and Lady MacBird. In her version, the two plotted to kill President Kennedy in order to intensify the war in Vietnam. Another well-known company, the Bread and Puppet Theater founded by Peter Schumann, used massive puppets and guerrilla theater to illustrate political protest ideas in the streets and on campuses across the country.

Off-Broadway Goes On

Even traditional theater began to feel the influence of modern cultural trends. In

A portable curtain sets the stage in Haight-Ashbury for the San Francisco Mime Troupe on July 1, 1967.

1959 Lorraine Hansberry became the first black woman playwright to have her work produced on Broadway. *Raisin in the Sun,* about an African American family's struggle to make a better life and buy a home in an all-white neighborhood in Chicago, won the New York Drama Critics' Circle Award for best play of 1959. Made into a well-known movie with Sidney Poitier in 1961, *Raisin* won a special award at the Cannes Film Festival. Now a classic, it was remade for television in 1991.

The plot and rock musical score of *Hair* put a new twist on traditional musicals. Written by Gerome Ragni and James Rado, *Hair* opened off-Broadway in 1967. It portrays a young man who is going to fight in a war but is deterred by a tribe of hippies, who manage to "save" him. One of the first Broadway productions to use a rock music score, the show sported just enough nudity to shock and intrigue audiences of the late sixties. *Hair* moved to Broadway the following year and was extremely popular, playing 1,750 performances before closing. As the title song pointed out, hair was still a major—if somewhat petty—issue in the continuing argument between the generations as the sixties came to a climax.

While Broadway and other traditional entertainment venues continued, Americans now had more drama choices than ever before as television entertained and guerrilla street theater expressed antiwar and other themes for free.

The Summer of Love
Against the backdrop of an escalating war in Vietnam and increasingly embattled civil rights protests, poet Allen Ginsberg toured college campuses where he sold out to huge crowds by joining others in calling for the Summer of Love in 1967. The Summer of Love was a national hippie celebration of life, imagination, love, and expanded consciousness through the use of marijuana, LSD, meditation, chanting, and whatever else "turned people on" to loving humanity and oneself with equal joy.

Allen Ginsberg mixes his poetic vision with politics and protest as he leads a pro-marijuana demonstration on February 11, 1965.

Middle-aged Ginsberg recited his poetry to thousands, accompanied by the rhythm of his finger cymbals and hypnotic chants, and stayed on campuses to celebrate with students for days afterward. His poem *Howl*, first performed in 1956, was an epic-length scream against the values of the fifties, and became a rallying cry not only for his own 1950s Beat generation but for the sixties counterculture. His *Kaddish and Other Poems 1958–60* brought the insights of Judaism and Zen Buddhism together with Walt Whitman's free verse and Jack Kerouac's prose to glorify the spiritual importance of everyday experience.

Novelists Influence a Generation

Novelists functioned as social commentators and agents of change more than ever in the sixties. Some of the most influential novels of the time were from older authors that baby boomers loved, such as Joseph Heller. His *Catch 22* focused on the absurd contradictions of the military in World War II and the insanity of war in any age. Other bestsellers of the time were Ken Kesey's *One Flew Over the Cuckoo's Nest*, Kurt Vonnegut's *Slaughterhouse Five*, Harper Lee's *To Kill a Mockingbird*, and Norman Mailer's novels, including his 1968 Pulitzer Prize–winning description of the 1967 peace march in Washington, D.C., *The Armies of the Night*. Heller,

Vonnegut, and Mailer explored war's contradictions, insanity, and deep tragedy with insight and biting humor. Ken Kesey was a baby boomer who most often traveled, in Richard Neville's words, "with his Merry Pranksters and Hell's Angels speeding . . . in that radiant International Harvester school bus, believed to be powered with LSD."[34] Kesey's book exposed the power struggles within an insane asylum, and the ugly side of a society that strives for rigid control at the expense of life and freedom. Harper Lee, much more reserved than the hippie hero Kesey, examined love and racial injustice in a poignant novel that won her a Pulitzer Prize, *To Kill a Mockingbird*.

On the less serious side, the comics of R. Crumb took cartoon characters beyond superheroes and *Archie and Veronica*, to the psychedelic-influenced *Zapp Comix*, starting in 1967. Crumb also created *Fritz the Cat, Head Comix*, and *Motor City Comics*, all of which reflected hippie counterculture values.

Movies

Movies of the time ranged from traditional musicals and epics such as *The Sound of Music, Patton*, and *Lawrence of Arabia* to films as bizarre as *Dr. Strangelove*. Released in 1964, *Strangelove* starred Peter Sellers as a mad Nazi-like scientist and climaxed with an American pilot riding a launched nuclear bomb as if it were a bucking bronco, shouting "Yippie!" as he plunged toward the Soviet Union. The film's subtitle, *How I Learned to Stop Worrying and Love the Bomb,* was something sixties moviegoers truly wanted to be able to do. *Strangelove* mocked the arms race and made audiences howl with laughter at a time when nuclear war was a very real fear.

The Graduate, released in 1968, captured the disconnection between young college graduates and their par-

ents. The movie used popular music, including Simon and Garfunkel's "Mrs. Robinson," to give voice to the younger generation's dismay at their parents' values and choices. College students flocked to it and made it a big hit. Musicals such as *My Fair Lady* (1964) starring Audrey Hepburn, and *The Sound of Music* (1965), starring Julie Andrews, one of the most popular family movies ever made, were big box-office draws.

The John Wayne film *The Green Berets* attracted those who supported

Dustin Hoffman plays a character seduced by Anne Bancroft in the movie The Graduate.

the war in Vietnam and frustrated those who were against it. John Wayne's son, Mike Wayne, produced and defended the movie:

> I'm not making a picture about Vietnam, I'm making a picture about good against bad. I happen to think that that's true about Vietnam, but even if it isn't as clear as all that, that's what you have to do to make a picture. It's all right, because we're in the business of selling tickets. It's the same thing as the Indians. Maybe we shouldn't have destroyed all those Indians, I don't know, but when you're making a picture, the Indians are the bad guys.[35]

By this time, much of the American public did not think "the Indians are the bad guys," even if this idea did sell tickets. Increasingly, movie makers faced the problem of offending some members of their audience if they relied on the old good guy–bad guy formula for making movies.

Television

CBS dominated television during the decade, airing thirteen out of the fifteen most popular shows, including personality-named variety and comedy shows starring Ed Sullivan, Lucille Ball, Jackie Gleason, Red Skelton, Andy Griffith, Dick Van Dyke, and Danny Thomas.

CBS also produced *The Beverly Hillbillies, Candid Camera, Family Affair*, and *Rawhide*. NBC enjoyed good ratings with the western *Bonanza* and *Laugh-In*, while ABC had a strong response to *Bewitched*. These shows amused, entertained, and continued to reflect a certain innocence. Foul language was strictly prohibited and sex did not play a major role in any of these shows. Most were family entertainment with formula plots punctuated by commercials. Watching TV, it was difficult to imagine that any Americans were discontent with their way of life.

Television Promotes Satire but Ignores Diversity

In this contented atmosphere, the spirit of irreverence and political satire, mildly apparent in the fifties in the work of such comedians as Steve Allen and Ernie Kovacs, increased in the sixties: By 1967, *The Smothers Brothers,* a weekly variety hour, combined innocent humor and "Yo-Yo Man's" silly yo-yo tricks with political humor and slightly racy jokes. Over the next two years, the brothers increased their attacks on the war in Vietnam, and, in 1969, with its ratings dropping, network censors cut the show off.

In a similar vein, *Laugh-In*, starring Dan Rowan and Dick Martin and featuring Goldie Hawn and Lily Tomlin, had a five-year run starting in 1967. It also

The hosts of Laugh-In, *Dan Rowan (far left) and Dick Martin, listen in as Goldie Hawn jokes with Arte Johnson (far right).*

an odd cast of characters. They also used a stage set with many windows and doors, which actors would open and slam shut when they took turns firing off their lines. Lily Tomlin invented a variety of characters for herself, including a power-mad telephone operator, with whom she poked fun at the monopoly Bell Telephone. Rowan and Martin always ended the show with Rowan telling Martin, "Say Goodnight, Dick," to which Dick Martin would reply "Goodnight, Dick."

Although *Laugh-In* and *The Smothers Brothers* were controversial, they were still for and about a white, middle-class audience. When African Americans and other minorities looked in the powerful mirror of television, they rarely saw themselves. There were virtually no nationally televised situation comedies or dramas starring people of color in the sixties, with rare exceptions such as Diahann Caroll in *Julia,* first aired in 1968. Situation comedies still showed only white, middle-class families with stay-at-home moms. National broadcasts blurred or erased

used political humor to amuse audiences and highlighted social issues of the time. The television camera zoomed in on conversations at a party to provide the groundbreaking format for one-liner jokes and opinions expressed between some regional differences but still ignored racial and cultural diversity, as well as economic differences among people. This made African Americans, other minorities, and the poor feel invisible. Sammy Davis Jr. and other black entertainers were merely "guests" on white shows, although they occasionally hosted their own "specials."

Women were generally portrayed within strict feminine stereotypes. An exception to this was comedian Phyllis Diller. She had a startling laugh that did not fit the standard of femininity, and poked fun at her housewife status with derogatory stories about her husband, "Fang."

Music Reflects Cultural Diversity

Music, in contrast to television, demonstrated the tremendous variety of cultural influences and styles that were actually available in the United States. As the cultural tastes of the decade became dominated by the country's biggest demographic group, the baby boomers' favorite music exploded in variety. This generation often walked right past the white music they were "supposed" to buy to get to rhythm and blues, soul, and other black music. Rock 'n' roll became the most popular genre, but country, rock-a-billy, folk, blues, rhythm and blues, soul, jazz, gospel, Motown, and California surfer music, to name the biggest musical trends, all found air time and an audience, challenging conventions and often making older generations complain about the "noise."

Rock 'n' Roll Dances to the Top of the Charts

Rock 'n' roll melded country, rhythm and blues, and gospel together into a sound that was vibrant and alive. Dances such as the Watusi, the Chicken, the Jerk, the Hitchhiker, and the Pony, as well as the Slop, the Mashed Potatoes, the Limbo, the Frug, the Swim, and the Stroll all got kids out on the dance floor. All paled in popularity, however, compared with the Twist.

Before it could become a national dance craze, the Twist had to win mainstream approval to be acceptable to the white middle class. Dick Clark, of television's *American Bandstand*, was the man to make this happen. His afterschool show, watched daily by 20 million fans, broadcast rock 'n' roll coast to coast in the fifties and sixties, and helped make it popular. The show periodically showcased black singers, but usually only if they fit white, Anglo-Saxon Protestant (WASP) cultural standards. Some, like Chubby Checker, could imitate other singers well enough to make big hits out of songs originally by less acceptable singers, like Hank Ballard and Elvis Presley, both of whom were too wild for the *Bandstand*. In 1960, Checker took Hank Ballard's *The Twist* and turned it into the number-one song in the nation. Ballard, who later made *Finger Poppin' Time* his own hit, took the royalties from *The Twist* for writing the song.

"Twisting" required very little foot-work, a big advantage for poor dancers. In this sense, it was a dance that even the clumsy could do. Chubby Checker's 1962 album from Cameo-Parkway Records listed "The Lose Your Inhibitions Twist" as the first song, and added the caution: "Adults Twist at Your Own Risk!" The cover claims,

> Not in the past fifty years has any dance completely captivated the en-tire world as has the TWIST. From Tokyo, Hong Kong, Paris, London and New York the TWIST has be-come the national dance craze. . . . There are even reports that they are twisting behind the Iron Curtain.[36]

An international fad, one of the first connections of the international youth culture, the Twist could be done alongside a partner, in a group, or on one's own.

The British Invasion

Music, more than any other medium, was tying the youth of the world to-

Chubby Checker put his own spin on Joey Dee and Henry Glover's Peppermint Twist, *first performed by Joey Dee and the Starliters.*

gether. In the early sixties, some U.S. radio stations (such as the all-black WLAC from Nashville, Tennessee) had a broad band that could be heard across much of the country. In all major cities, blacks moving north got "their" music on the low end of the dial in most areas. But radio receivers did not discriminate. Searching for good music on their radio dial, many whites tuned in, and liked what they heard.

The Beatles, the Rolling Stones, and other British rock groups such as the Who and the Animals listened to the black roots of American music and then brought it back to the United States with a British twist. By 1964, just when the United States was getting bored with bland, Dick Clark–style rock 'n' roll, the British invaded with their own high-energy version. American teens were electrified.

The Rolling Stones, named after a song by blues master Muddy Waters, played more "cover" music, or music first made famous by another group, than the Beatles did. At first the Stones just took black groups' songs and performed them, rather than writing their own. Soon, however, they were combining blues with the black rock sound of Chuck Berry and others to create a vibrant sound all their own.

The Beatles combined the distinct sounds of Chuck Berry, Little Richard, Elvis Presley, and others and shaped a sound that dominated the sixties with its creativity and style. They had exploded onto the international music world in 1961, causing a sensation called Beatlemania wherever they went. The amazingly energetic, charming group released eighteen increasingly complex record albums in the seven years from 1963 to 1970. They also acted and sang in four live-action movies: *A Hard Day's Night* (1964), *Help!* (1965), *Magical Mystery Tour* (1968), and *Let It Be* (1970). The albums

Soul Music with a British Accent

The British had to work even harder than Americans to find American black gospel, soul, and rock 'n' roll on the radio or in record shops. Their government controlled nearly all national radio and TV broadcast outlets and chose most of what the British saw or heard. In the fifties and sixties, very little British air time was devoted to the American fad called rock 'n' roll. As Keith Richards of the Rolling Stones recalls in *The Rolling Stones*, "Jazz and classical. That's all I remember from the BBC in the '50s. That's what you grew up knowing."

Yet somehow, from record shops to short-wave radio, many British youth managed to hear Americans Bill Haley, Buddy Holly, Elvis Presley, Little Richard, and real rhythm and blues. Touring Europe, rock 'n' roll greats such as Chuck Berry and Bo Diddley were more popular in Britain than they were in the United States.

It was this love of American music, and especially black music, that gave the British invasion its unique energy and sound. British groups listened to African American music and brought it back to America with a European twist that gave it a unique appeal worldwide.

The Beatles join the "British invasion" and first conquer the United States with their music and "mop top" hair in 1964.

and their movies show their evolution from "lads from Liverpool" through their exposure to drugs and the rewards of fame and fortune.

The music of British invasion rock groups reflected the growth of their greatest fans, the baby boom generation. The message of their music shifted as the counterculture became more revolutionary. The Beatles, for example, in "Revolution" seemed to many to have become disheartened, even disillusioned, with the counterculture of protest they had come to symbolize. They sang of the desire to change the world they shared with their generation but declared they wanted no part in violently tearing down the system:

"But if you go carrying pictures of Chairman Mao, you ain't gonna make it with anyone anyhow. . . ." [In the same vein] The Rolling Stones seemed frustrated at the lack of effective outlet for their own rebelliousness in "Street Fighting Man." They sang of summertime protests in the streets of London and yet [shared] a sense of their own helplessness to play an important role in response to injustices they saw: "But what can a poor boy do except sing for a rock 'n' roll band."[37]

New Words to Old-Time Music

Alongside the new music of the sixties, folksingers continued the traditions of the oldest American music: ballads, fiddle tunes, and love songs that immigrants had brought from the British Isles.

The focus of folk music was its message, and folksingers of the sixties expressed their views on war, racism, civil rights, justice, and the "establishment." Chief among its creators were Bob Dylan and Joan Baez, who continued the leftist folksinger tradition of

Payola and Watered Down Rock 'n' Roll

The Beatles entered the United States at a time when rock 'n' roll was becoming watered-down and bland. This was partly due to politics and profit, rather than available musical talent.

A congressional investigation into payola, or bribing disc jockeys to play certain records, had attacked rock 'n' roll and kept all but the most romantic, but asexual, versions off the air. Although the practice of payola was widespread throughout the music industry, those who promoted rhythm and blues artists and strong rock 'n' roll musicians were harassed more than others. In spite of practicing similar corruption, Dick Clark and his less raw, sweeter versions of rock 'n' roll were spared.

Clark financially invested in many of the records he played on his show, and profited from their popularity, but this conflict of interest was not exposed in the crackdown on payola. As the competition was swept away by congressional crackdowns, Clark's influence and watered-down version of rock 'n' roll thrived. Radio shows were dominated by the soft-sounding ballads of white teenagers like Shelley Fabares singing "Johnny Angel."

At the same time, as the decade began, many rock 'n' roll careers had hit hard times or turned away from the music: Elvis was in the army, Buddy Holly and Richie Valens were dead, and Little Richard had renounced rock 'n' roll and turned to religion instead. Teens were hungry for a rock group with energy and sex appeal. The Beatles and the Rolling Stones, whose idols were black American singers like Little Richard, fit the bill.

the thirties and forties by writing songs of protest and warning for the sixties.

Part of folk music's appeal was that folksingers continually created new songs to express the concerns of each new generation. Singer Pete Seeger's *Where Have all the Flowers Gone?* made such a strong antiwar statement that it made many young people question war for the first time. It became so popular it was played on the *Hit Parade* alongside rock 'n' roll's top hits of the day.

Another powerful hit song was Bob Dylan's *The Times They Are A-Changin'*, in which he warns senators, congressmen, and any others who want to stop the civil rights and peace movements that they should get out of the way if they can't lend a hand. Dylan also warned people about joining the military-industrial establishment in *Only a Pawn in Their Game*. Equally dedicated to the counterculture's agenda, Baez donated the proceeds from almost every concert she gave to a cause, from migrant farmworkers and civil rights to draft resis-

Bob Dylan and Joan Baez began their musical collaboration—and later romance—by singing "With God on Our Side" at the Monterey Folk Festival in May 1963.

tance and peace. She lived modestly, despite her fame and profits.

Motown Magic

Black influences increasingly broke into the mainstream, but they had to be carefully packaged in order to cross over to white audiences. Detroit's Motown label cleaned up "soul music" by making it more polished and simple than the raw, emotional gospel music from which it came. Berry Gordy Jr. started the Motown company in 1962 and launched the careers of such artists as Smokey Robinson and the Miracles, Little Stevie Wonder, The Jackson Five, and Diana Ross and the Supremes. To make these stars more acceptable to white audiences, he made them take lessons in etiquette and table manners, choreographed their moves on stage, backed their tunes with the string section of the Detroit symphony, and dressed his performers in evening clothes and carefully coifed wigs. Motown brought a new rhythm called the back beat that was driving but easy to dance to. By appealing to the white mainstream as well as blacks, he created the first successful black-owned record company in the nation. By 1980 it was also the largest.

Motown was eclipsed by the hard-edged Philadelphia sound, exemplified by such performers as Sly and Family Stone and the soul music of Aretha Franklin and James Brown, who brought his own raw scream and unusual beat as the sixties evolved. With soul music, Ray Charles brought the Mississippi Delta into northern living rooms, and Aretha Franklin brought the church choir and a Big Mama look.

Coming Together: Woodstock Nation

The musical finale of the sixties was a rock festival held in the summer of 1969 outside the little town of Bethel in the Catskill Mountain's area of New York. A large crowd was expected to assemble on August 15 for several days of music. When close to half a million people showed up, Woodstock Festival became Woodstock Nation, the largest "be-in" of the decade.

In many ways, Woodstock was a coming-of-age party for baby boomers. Crowds of counterculture youth flooded into the area, but despite the crush of people, most were relaxed and peaceful. Traffic jams forced people to get out and walk to the campsite. Abandoned cars made the highways impassable. Then it rained. Fields turned to mud. The organizers ran short of food, drinking water, toilet paper, and supplies in general. Instead of becoming angry and competitive, people shared with one another and enjoyed the music.

Many of the performances broke new musical ground. Jimi Hendrix turned ordinary melodies into strange and powerful improvisations with unusual sound experiments wove through them, trailblazing a new genre called acid rock. He played his guitar with his teeth, and mixed the sounds of air force bombers with the national anthem in a highly creative version that wordlessly protested the war in Vietnam. Janis Joplin laughed her inimitable cackle, sang *Bobby McGee,* and, when she crooned, "Oh Lord, won't you buy me a Mercedes Benz / My friends all have Porsches, I must make amends," the crowd sang along, smiling at her social commentary on their consumer society.

In spite of the overwhelming size of the crowd, there were no riots, and only one accidental death. Faced with many more people than they ever anticipated, the organizers brought in trucks of water to help take care of their needs. They hired helicopters to fly out people who were ill or overdosed on drugs. Woodstock Nation seemed a fitting climax to a decade that found its young people exploring alternative lifestyles. Many had tried to band together to end racial injustice and war, live in peace, and celebrate life. For a few days they could demon-

Jimi Hendrix took the guitar and rock music scene to a wild new dimension in his short lifetime.

strate their communal values, revel in their music, and give life to the Beatles' refrain, "All we are saying, is give peace a chance."

Chapter Seven

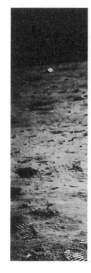

Buzz Aldrin shuffles across the lunar surface after the Apollo 11 *mission lands the first men on the moon on July 20, 1969.*

The Space Race and Technology Take Us to the Moon

Political upheavals and social change dominated the United States in the sixties. Yet perhaps the most important event of the decade, from a scientific and technological point of view, was that humanity finally launched itself off the planet and onto the moon. In the process, political and diplomatic efforts gradually moved the cold war away from nuclear confrontation and toward more international cooperation.

It was an icy moment in the cold war when the Soviets stunned the United States and bruised American national pride by launching the world's first artificial satellite into orbit around the earth, on October 4, 1957. With this vehicle, called *Sputnik I,* the Soviets jumped out of the starting gate and won the first lap in the space race. This was seen as a military threat that quickly became a cold war competition: "When the Russians launched the first intercontinental ballistic missile and Sputnik, in 1957, they blasted the national pride and stoked a national panic. Liberals flailed away, helpless to arrest the momentum of the arms race."[38] Anxious to catch up with their sworn enemy, the U.S. launched its own unmanned satellite, *Explorer I,* just four months later on January 31, 1958. The race was on, and the United States was determined to be a contender.

Some three years later, on April 12, 1961, the Soviets beat the United States again with another space first, rocketing Yuri Gagarin into an orbital space flight. The United States was determined to close the gap in the race: On May 5, 1961, Alan B. Shepard Jr. climbed into his *Mercury* capsule and made the first U.S. piloted suborbital space flight. The United States was not yet in orbit, but at least they had a man flying in space.

Politics, Not Science, Fuels Space Capsules

The largest leap forward in the space race did not come through advances in science or technology, but through politics. Americans in general were strongly patriotic, competitive, and used to winning on a global scale. Americans wanted to maintain their competitive position in the world militarily, scientifically, economically, and educationally. Steeped in the competition of the cold war, many were even willing to pay increased taxes to compete with the USSR. President Kennedy decided to take advantage of this mood and support an all-out effort to put an American on the moon. As scientist Carl Sagan, winner of the NASA Apollo Achievement Award, remembers:

> The scope and audacity of John Kennedy's May 25, 1961 message to a joint session of Congress on "Urgent National Needs"—the speech that launched the Apollo program—dazzled me. We would use rockets not yet designed and alloys not yet conceived, navigation and docking schemes not yet devised, in order to send a man to an unknown world—a world not yet explored, not even in a preliminary way, not even by robots—and we would bring him safely back, and we would do it before the decade was over. This confident pronouncement was made before any American had even achieved Earth orbit.

Kennedy tells a joint session of Congress that there is an "urgent national need" to pursue space exploration.

As a newly minted Ph.D., I actually thought all this had something centrally to do with science. But the President did not talk about discovering the origin of the Moon, or even about bringing samples of it back for study. All he seemed to be interested in was sending some-one there and bringing him home. It was a kind of *gesture*. . . .

The Apollo program is really about politics, others told me. This sounded more promising. Non-aligned nations would be tempted to drift toward the Soviet Union if it was ahead in space exploration, if the United States showed insufficient "national vigor." I didn't follow. Here was the United States, ahead of the Soviet Union in virtually every area of technology—the world's economic, military, and on occasion, even moral leader—and Indonesia would go Communist because Yuri Gagarin beat John Glenn to Earth orbit? What's so special about space technology? Suddenly I understood.

Sending people to orbit the Earth or robots to orbit the Sun requires rockets—big, reliable, powerful rockets. Those same rockets can be used for nuclear war. The same technology that transports a man to the Moon can carry nuclear warheads halfway around the world. The same technology that puts an astronomer and a telescope in Earth orbit can also put up a laser "battle station." Even back then, there was fanciful talk in military circles, East and West, about space as the new "high ground," about the nation that "controlled" space "controlling" the Earth. Of course strategic rockets were already being tested on Earth. But heaving a ballistic missile with a dummy warhead into a target zone in the middle of the Pacific Ocean doesn't buy

much glory. Sending people into space captures the attention and imagination of the world.[39]

The Choice: Military Competition or Explorer's Race?

Cold war politics fueled the first laps of the space race but Kennedy's vision of a lunar landing was one influence that helped shift the race away from a military approach. NASA's charter limited the agency to peaceful space exploration. Even so, since neither country was sure of its rival's true goals, both the United States and the Soviet Union pursued military objectives along with exploration of space throughout the sixties. For example, authors Erlend A. Kennan and Edmund H. Harvey Jr. note:

Out of NASA's new and zealous devotion to "limited warfare" problems came a bright idea for completely revolutionizing guerrilla warfare. The House Subcommittee on NASA Oversight boasted that NASA could loft a synchronous satellite over the Vietnam jungles—a satellite equipped with a huge mirror designed to reflect the sun's rays twenty-four hours a day. The satellite could be used to illuminate the darkened battle area, putting the enemy at a distinct and obvious disadvantage. Only the loud protests of civilian astronomers, concerned that their celestial observations would be hampered, seem to have quelled that unique idea.

One must ask, of course, had such a reflector been launched, were the North Vietnamese and their Soviet allies expected to leave it intact? Would we really have been surprised if Russia knocked it out of orbit, thus enacting the first hostile counter-maneuver in space?[40]

From this and other examples we can see that although the space race was politically driven, the road of military confrontation was avoided and gradually exploration won out. The Apollo program initiated by President Kennedy took funds away from other Defense Department space projects that never reached completion, including orbiting platforms that carried robot weapons aimed at enemy satellites and ballistic missiles, and vehicles to put military personnel in orbit. The Apollo program also drained money from strictly scientific projects in space while it focused on landing an American on the moon. The scientific community

grumbled and complained, but also tried to add their experiments to the Apollo space program whenever they could.

Before Americans could use space as a laboratory for either scientific or military purposes, they had to achieve manned orbit. On February 20, 1962, John H. Glenn Jr. became the first American in orbit when he circled Earth three times in his *Friendship 7* space capsule. The name of the capsule series emphasized a goal of cooperation rather than war. Glenn's achievement helped Americans feel more secure about their ability to compete with the Soviets in space, at least on this level.

Astronaut John Glenn prepares to orbit the earth, lowering himself into the Friendship 7 *space capsule on Cape Canaveral, Florida, on February 20, 1962.*

Space Diplomacy on the Ground

At the same time, U.S. diplomats pursued nuclear arms agreements and resolutions that would lessen the dangers of war on earth and keep nuclear weapons out of the heavens. Frank B. Gibney and George J. Feldman explain:

> On a political level the United States repeatedly pledged itself not to use the space dimension for military purposes. At the Geneva disarmament talks and at the UN, the American delegates assured everyone who would listen that this country would not orbit weapons of mass destruction in space, provided of course that the Russians refrained from so doing. The test-ban treaty of August 5, 1963, specifically outlawed nuclear-weapon testing in outer space. U.S. diplomats have continued to underscore the policy laid down by John F. Kennedy in his speech to the UN General Assembly in September, 1963, that "we must continue to seek agreement . . . on an arrangement to keep weapons of mass destruction out of outer space."[41]

Firsts in Space

Soviet firsts in the space race are impressive. They include the first human in space and first human to orbit the earth, both on *Vostok 1* in 1961. The Soviets also gave us the first spacecraft to fly by other planets (*Venera 1* to Venus in 1961, and *Mars 1* to Mars in 1962) and the first woman in space, Valentina Tereshkova, who orbited the earth for more than seventy hours in *Vostok 6* in 1963. These achievements were followed by the first multiperson space mission (*Voskhod 1*, 1964) and the first "space walk," from *Voskhod 2* in 1965. By this time, the United States had made the first scientifically successful planetary mission (*Mariner 2* to Venus) and put the first astronomical observatory in space (OSO-1).

Then the Soviet Union launched the first spacecraft to enter the atmosphere of another planet, sending *Venera 3* through the thick sulfuric acid atmosphere of Venus, and made their *Luna 10* the first spacecraft to orbit another world, orbiting the moon in 1966. They continued to speed ahead in the space race by making the first successful soft landing on another world with *Luna 9*, landing an unmanned craft on the moon in 1966.

With this, the Soviets had reached the moon by remote control. In second place, the United States rushed to be the first country to arrive on the moon in person. They achieved a manned orbit of the moon with astronauts Frank Borman, William A. Anders, and James A. Lovell Jr. onboard in 1968. Finally,

Haste Creates Tragedy

NASA officials were in a hurry to get Apollo launched. Instead of returning a badly flawed first command module, NASA made at least 623 changes to spacecraft 012 in an attempt to get it ready for space. In spite of all these needed corrections to the original design, astronauts Gus Grissom, Ed White, and Roger Chaffee were sealed inside the hatch for a launching drill on January 27, 1966. After five and a half hours, during which their pressurized cabin was filled to 16 psi with pure oxygen to prevent nitrogen leaks, the simulated countdown was stopped at T-10 minutes. Then Chaffee reported matter-of-factly: "Fire, I smell fire."

The astronauts moved quickly to use evacuation procedures, but within sixteen seconds the spacecraft cabin exploded. It took five more minutes for the hatches to be removed, by which time all three astronauts were not only dead from asphyxiation, but scorched and welded to the melted electrical insulation and other flammable materials of the spacecraft.

Before the disaster, Ed White, Roger Chaffee, and Gus Grissom check operating systems in Apollo.

After this tragedy, it took two more years before a new command module passed all the safety tests designed to prevent a repeat of this accident. The new hatch opened outward instead of inward, and could be opened in ten seconds instead of the 90 seconds required to open the original two hatches. Pure oxygen, highly flammable, was not used until the craft was safe in the vacuum of space, and future crews were issued fire-resistant clothing.

on July 20, 1969, Kennedy's goal of reaching the moon by the end of the decade was fulfilled.

Detaching their landing module from the *Apollo 11,* astronauts Edwin E.

"Buzz" Aldrin Jr. and Neil Armstrong landed the Eagle in the moon's Sea of Tranquility at 4:18 EDT. Astronaut Neil Armstrong radioed mission control in Texas, "Houston . . . Tranquillity Base here. The Eagle has landed."[42] While Michael Collins circled the moon in the command module of *Apollo 11* and Aldrin waited behind him in the landing module, Armstrong carefully stepped through the lunar module door. He pulled a D-ring to expose a television camera that would transmit his first step onto the moon to a billion viewers, about one-fifth of the earth's human population. Farther away from home than any explorer had ever been in the history of humanity, he was connected through television—in another historical first—to his family, country, and the world community: "I'm at the foot of the ladder," he reported. "The surface appears to be very, very fine-grained as you get close to it. It's almost like a powder." At 10:56 EDT he placed his left boot onto this lunar soil and pronounced the historic words, "That's one small step for man, one giant leap for mankind."[43] Again, the whole world was watching.

The peaceful intent of the mission was emphasized by the plaque the astronauts left behind. The words were a stark contrast to events on earth, where the United States continued to wage war in Vietnam. As Carl Sagan remembers:

For me, the most ironic token of that moment in history is the plaque signed by President Richard M. Nixon that *Apollo 11* took to the moon. It reads: "We came in peace for all mankind." As the United States was dropping 7½ megatons of conventional explosives on small nations in Southeast Asia, we congratulated ourselves on our humanity: We would harm no one on a lifeless rock. That plaque is there still, attached to the base of *Apollo 11* Lunar Module, on the airless desolation of the Sea of Tranquility. If no one disturbs it, it will still be readable a million years from now.[44]

As ironic as that plaque seemed to some, it marked an effort, however feeble, to point the space race away from the military confrontations still raging on earth. It was a political gesture on a political journey, but it was witnessed by a world suddenly united by a new reality: they were one family, humanity, from the planet Earth. They had landed on the moon.

Unlike explorers in previous generations, the explorers of what was now officially the space age did not claim the moon as their property. Although the mission planted the U.S. flag on the moon in the tradition of explorers who claimed new lands for their king or country, no speech was made to claim the moon for the

Political Display

Landing people on the moon was both a technological and political victory. Bringing them home again was a great political triumph, and the U.S. government made the most of it, as William B. Breuer describes in his 1993 book *Race to the Moon: America's Duel with the Soviets:*

On the flight deck awaiting the moon men's arrival was President Nixon, who had winged nearly 7,000 miles from Washington on the first leg of a world trip in order personally to greet America's newest legends. . . . Beaming broadly and freshly shaven, Neil Armstrong, Buzz Aldrin, and Michael Collins emerged from the chopper; the band broke into the designated tune, and a few thousand sailors stirred up waves with rousing cheers. The tumultuous reception was short-lived: the three astronauts, on the slight chance that they might carry moon germs, were hustled into a mobile quarantine van.

"We learned how monkeys in a cage feel," Collins would quip.

President Nixon approached the van and could not disguise his awe and enthusiasm about conversing with men on the other side of the glass who had just returned from the moon. In a fit of buoyancy, Nixon exclaimed: "This is the greatest week in the history of the world since the Creation!"

. . . The quarantine van holding Neil Armstrong, Buzz Aldrin, and Michael Collins was unloaded from the *Hornet* at Pearl Harbor, Hawaii, and then flown to the Manned Spacecraft Center in Houston. There

Back from the moon, Neil Armstrong, Michael Collins, and Buzz Aldrin are welcomed with a New York City ticker tape parade in 1969.

the astronauts and their precious cargo of moon rocks and soil were transferred into an 83,000 square foot lunar receiving laboratory.

After 18 days "in custody" (as Michael Collins described it), the three moon men were given conquering heroes' parades in New York City, Chicago, and Los Angeles. Then, flying in the presidential jet, *Air Force One*, they went on a 45-day, 24-nation goodwill tour that focused the world spotlight on America's superiority in science and technology. In the cold war that was raging globally, it was a victory march.

United States. Who could try to own the moon? To do so would be both absurd and dangerous, provoking war and worldwide disapproval. By stepping onto another world, Americans found themselves working with a new dimension: the dimension of infinite space. Space was so vast, so overwhelming to the small humans shooting themselves into it, that it humbled even the proudest of nations. Clearly, space was meant to be shared.

Technology Gets a Boost

The space race pulled scientists and technicians from every discipline: rocket scientists and geologists, climatologists and cosmologists, electricians and engineers, astronomers and biologists. They worked singly and in teams. Combining their ideas and knowledge in new ways, they created a space industry that used technologies that had been developing independently in private industry. In turn, the space industry gave the world new products and technology, from powdered "orange juice" called Tang® and Velcro® closures to communication satellites such as *Echo I*, the world's first communication satellite, launched in 1960.

Scientists Finally Allowed on Moon

In the six moon landings that followed the first manned lunar landing, only the last one finally carried an actual scientist, geologist Harrison H. Schmitt. He and others noted scientific and economic reasons for returning to the moon. Schmitt is quoted in *Moon Missions:*

Helium-3 was discovered in the lunar soil samples brought back to Earth from the Apollo missions. Although present in concentrations of only 20 to 30 parts per billion, it is far more accessible on the Moon than on our own planet. An almost limitless supply is believed to exist in the upper several meters of pulverized rock on the lunar surface.

Relatively small amounts of helium-3, mined and processed on the Moon, then transported to Earth for use in fusion power plants, could produce enormous amounts of energy. . . . Another benefit of replacing oil-burning power plants with fusion plants would be global reductions in the emission of pollutants.

This is not a fantastic dream. It is a viable commercial option to meet the energy demands of the 21st Century. As the world population expands, and economic aspirations grow, alternatives must be found to the continued depletion of fossil fuels. While the creation of a space transportation infrastructure, lunar mining and processing facilities, and terrestrial power plants represents a formidable challenge, so did the Apollo Program.

Winning the space race to the moon was a symbolic victory for the U.S. capitalist system, where private industry paid for research, joined in partnership with government programs, and profited. The Soviet Communist system of government-owned and operated technology and industry had fallen short of walking on the moon, but it had achieved many technological advances. As space exploration continued, the two competing systems increasingly joined in cooperative ventures to save money, combine expertise, and promote friendship between the United States and the USSR.

The Birth of Computers

The sixties were years of other great technological leaps forward. Often, one invention or discovery would spark advances in several industries at once. This was especially true of the computer industry, which was just in its infancy. For example, in 1958, Jack Kilby created the first integrated circuit for Texas Instruments. The first minicomputer was introduced by Digital Equipment Corporation in 1963. It was not until 1968 that the first random-access memory (RAM) system was put in operation. This finally allowed immediate access to information from anywhere within a computer's memory. As computers became smarter and faster, many industries began to apply them to their own needs.

Many corporations, including Bell Telephone, had huge private research facilities devoted to advances in lasers, computers, transistors, and other research. For example, before Erna Schneider Hoover of Bell Laboratories developed and patented the first computer software used to switch telephone calls, telephone switches were controlled by electromechanical relay equipment. Telephone calls were processed by selecting bars that physically connected with holding bars, or, in advanced systems, by computer-operated mechanical switches. Hoover's software, some of the first to be patented, measured the number of calls a system received. It then redirected calls to avoid overloading the system. Hoover worked with a team at Bell Labs for years in order to develop the first electronic switching system in 1965. The team created a programmable digital computer to control the switching network.

Winning the Race, Learning to Cooperate

Despite the competitive nature of the race, space exploration brought increased international cooperation on many levels. It also gave people around the world a new perspective. For the first time, Americans and people all over the world saw photographs of their own planet from space. It was now possible to imagine humanity as a community of travelers, all aboard "spaceship earth." As the sixties ended, the earth seemed tiny and delicate, a small home planet spinning in the vast emptiness of space. The United States had stamped the decade with its unique brand of progress and controversy, culture, and communication. The space age had been launched. With it, the need to find peaceful solutions to controversy at home and abroad became more important than ever.

Notes

Chapter One:
Cold War and the End of Camelot

1. Michael R. Beschloss, *Mayday*. New York: Harper & Row, 1986, p. 59.
2. Quoted in Beschloss, *Mayday*, pp. 262–63.
3. Quoted in Ernest R. May and Philip D. Zelikow, eds., *The Kennedy Tapes: Inside the White House During the Cuban Missile Crisis*. Cambridge, MA: Belknap Press of Harvard University Press, 1997, p. 222.
4. Quoted in 101st Congress, 1st Session, Senate Document 101-10, *Inaugural Addresses of the Presidents of the United States, from George Washington 1789 to George Bush 1989*. Bicentennial Edition. Washington, DC: U.S. Government Printing Office, 1989, p. 308.
5. Quoted in Harris Wofford, *Of Kennedys and Kings: Making Sense of the Sixties*. Pittsburgh: University of Pittsburgh Press, 1980, p. 173.

Chapter Two: Guns and Butter:
Politics in the 1960s

6. Quoted in Glenn R. Capp, *The Great Society*. Belmont, CA: Dickenson, 1967, p. 18.

7. Quoted in Capp, *The Great Society*, p. 176.
8. Quoted in Capp, *The Great Society*, p. 176.
9. Quoted in Capp, *The Great Society*, p. 21.
10. Quoted in Capp, *The Great Society*, p. 177.
11. Quoted in Capp, *The Great Society*, p. 20.
12. J. Evetts Haley, *A Texan Looks at Lyndon: A Study in Illegitimate Power*. Canyon, TX: Palo Duro Press, 1964, p. 11.

Chapter Three: The Vietnam War
and Johnson's Great Society

13. Quoted in Capp, *The Great Society*, p. 20.
14. Quoted in James Olson and Randy Roberts, *Where the Domino Fell: America and Vietnam, 1945–1990*. New York: St. Martin's Press, 1991, p. 43.
15. Quoted in Neil Sheehan, *A Bright and Shining Lie: John Paul Vann and America in Vietnam*. New York: Vintage, 1988, p. 589.
16. Quoted in Alexander Bloom and Wini Breines, eds., *"Takin' It to the Streets": A Sixties Reader*. New York:

Oxford University Press, 1995, p. 323.

17. Quoted in Bloom and Breines, *"Takin' It to the Streets,"* p. 251.

18. Quoted in Edwin O. Guthman and C. Richard Allen, eds., *RFK Collected Speeches.* New York: Viking, 1993, p. 294.

19. Quoted in Guthman and Allen, *RFK Collected Speeches,* p. 292.

20. Quoted in Guthman and Allen, *RFK Collected Speeches*, p. 294.

Chapter Four: Civil Rights: The Quest for Equality

21. Taylor Branch, *Pillar of Fire: America in the King Years 1963–65.* New York: Simon and Schuster, 1998, p. 122.

22. Quoted in Wil A. Linkugel, ed., *Contemporary American Speeches: A Sourcebook of Speech Forms and Principles.* 3rd ed. Belmont, CA: Wadsworth, 1972, p. 291.

23. Quoted in Branch, *Pillar of Fire,* p. 230.

24. Quoted in Branch, *Pillar of Fire,* p. 364.

25. Quoted in Michael R. Beschloss, ed., *Taking Charge: The Johnson White House Tapes, 1963–64.* New York: Simon and Schuster, 1997, p. 427.

26. Quoted in Branch, *Pillar of Fire,* p. 373.

27. Quoted in Branch, *Pillar of Fire,* p. 178.

Chapter Five: Countercultures Provide Alternatives

28. Gene Anthony, *Summer of Love.* Millbrae, CA: Celestial Arts, 1980, p. 66.

29. Quoted in Anthony, *Summer of Love,* p. 76.

30. William Burroughs, *Naked Lunch.* Paris: Olympia Press, 1959, p. 74.

31. Quoted in Bloom and Breines, *"Takin' It to the Streets,"* p. 408.

32. Betty Friedan, *It Changed My Life.* New York: Random House, 1976, p. xiii.

Chapter Six: Arts and Entertainment Reflect the Counterculture

33. Yoko Ono, *Grapefruit.* New York: Simon and Schuster, 1970, n.p.

34. Richard Neville, *Play Power: Exploring the International Underground.* New York: Random House, 1970, p. 35.

35. Quoted in Edward Sorel, *Making the World Safe for Hypocrisy.* Chicago: Swallow Press, 1972, p. 43.

36. Album cover, *Chubby Checker for 'Teen Twisters Only.* Philadelphia: Cameo–Parkway Records, 1962.

37. Jules Witcover, *The Year the Dream Died.* New York: Warner Books, 1997, p. 460.

Chapter Seven: The Space Race and Technology Take Us to the Moon

38. Todd Gitlin, *The Sixties: Years of Hope, Days of Rage.* New York: Bantam Books, 1987, p. 86.

39. Carl Sagan, *Pale Blue Dot: A Vision of the Human Future in Space.* New York: Random House, 1994, p. 209.

40. Erlend A. Kennan and Edmund H. Harvey Jr., *Mission to the Moon: A Critical Examination of NASA and the Space Program.* New York: William Morrow, 1969, p. 209.

41. Frank B. Gibney and George J. Feldman, *The Reluctant Space-Farers.* New York: New American Library of World Literature, 1965, p. 93.

42. Quoted in William F. Melberg, *Moon Missions: Mankind's First Voyages to Another World.* Plymouth, MI: Plymouth Press, 1997, p. 92.

43. Quoted in Melberg, *Moon Missions,* p. 94.

44. Sagan, *Pale Blue Dot,* p. 212.

Chronology

1960

February 1: Four African American college students attempt to integrate a Woolworth lunch counter in Greensboro, North Carolina, beginning a sit-in after being denied service.

April 21: Congress passes a landmark voting rights act.

May 1: American U2 spy plane is shot down over Soviet Union and pilot Gary Powers is captured; President Eisenhower's administration is soon caught lying about the plane's purpose. As a result, a summit conference in Paris crumbles.

May 9: The birth control pill is approved for use in the United States.

September 26: John F. Kennedy and Richard M. Nixon face each other in the nation's first televised presidential debate.

1961

January 3: The United States cuts off diplomatic relations with Cuba.

January 20: John F. Kennedy is sworn in as the thirty-fifth president of the United States.

April 12: Yuri Gagarin, Soviet cosmonaut, becomes the first human to orbit the earth and travel in space.

April 17: The Central Intelligence Agency backs Cuban exiles' disastrous invasion of Cuba at the Bay of Pigs in a humiliating defeat for the United Sates.

May 5: Alan B. Shepard becomes the first American to achieve a suborbital space flight.

May 14: A busload of African American and white Freedom Riders are ambushed and beaten by a white mob near Anniston, Alabama, as they attempt to travel through the south to New Orleans. They are part of the Freedom Ride campaign to monitor southern desegregation, which continues throughout the summer.

August 13: The Soviets erect the Berlin Wall through the center of the German city, intensifying the cold war.

1962

February 14: President Kennedy orders his U.S. military advisers in Vietnam to return fire if fired upon.

February 20: John H. Glenn Jr. becomes the first American in orbit as he circles the earth three times in the U.S. *Friendship 7* space capsule.

October 1: James Meredith becomes the first black student to enroll at the University of Mississippi, supported by three thousand federal troops needed to put down anti-integration riots.

October 22: The Cuban missile crisis begins and the United States goes on wartime alert as President Kennedy announces that an American U2 spy plane took pictures of Soviet nuclear missile installations in Cuba.

October 28: Kennedy and Soviet premier Nikita Khrushchev end the Cuban missile crisis with an agreement to have the Soviet missiles dismantled.

December: The modern environmental movement is launched with the release of Rachel Carson's book of warning, *Silent Spring*.

1963

Betty Friedan sparks the beginning of the modern feminist movement, publishing *The Feminine Mystique*.

June 17: The Supreme Court rules that laws requiring students to recite school prayers or biblical verses are unconstitutional.

August 28: The landmark March on Washington is nationally televised, bringing Dr. Martin Luther King Jr.'s "I Have a Dream" speech—and demands for equal rights for African Americans—to the entire country.

November 22: President Kennedy is fatally shot in Dallas, Texas; Vice President Lyndon Johnson is sworn in as president, and the country goes into mourning.

November 24: Kennedy's suspected murderer, Lee Harvey Oswald, is shot and killed on live national television by Jack Ruby, a Dallas nightclub owner.

1964

February: The Beatles land in America, met by hysterical fans.

Summer: All major civil rights groups join to register African American voters during what was called the Freedom Summer.

June 23: Three civil rights voter-registration workers are reported missing in Mississippi. President Johnson orders FBI director J. Edgar Hoover to send agents, who finally find their bodies in August.

July 2: Johnson signs the landmark Civil Rights Act, banning racial discrimination in voting, jobs, public accommodations, and federally funded programs and projects.

August 7: Congress approves presidential military action in Vietnam with the Tonkin Resolution.

August 11: Congress passes Johnson's War on Poverty bill.

September 27: The Warren Commission declares that Lee Harvey Oswald acted alone when he assassinated President Kennedy. Questions of possible conspiracy continue in spite of this report.

1965

February: The United States begins continuous bombing of North Vietnam.

February 21: Malcolm X, the Black Muslim leader who had split with Elijah Muhammad, is murdered in New York City.

July 30: Medicare goes into effect, providing a medical safety net for American elderly.

August 6: President Johnson signs a new Voting Rights Act, prohibiting states from using literacy tests and poll taxes to limit minority voter registration.

August 11: Riots begin in the Watts area of Los Angeles, causing thirty-four deaths and over $200 million in damages.

September 21: Congress passes the Water Quality Act, designed to reduce water pollution.

October 3: Immigration quotas by ethnic origin are abolished by the Immigration Act. This raises quotas for the Western Hemisphere to 120,000, and immigrants from other countries to 170,000. President Johnson encourages refugees from oppressive governments to seek a new home in the United States.

1966

The National Organization for Women (NOW) is founded, led by Betty Friedan, to establish "full equality for women in America in a truly equal partnership with men."

March: Cesar Chavez wins the first migrant worker labor contract in the history of the U.S. labor movement.

May 1: The United States pursues Vi-

etcong and North Vietnamese soldiers into neighboring Cambodia, widening the war.

June 29: The United States begins bombing the North Vietnamese capital, Hanoi.

1967

January 27: Three U.S. astronauts, Edward J. White Jr., Virgil I. Grissom, and Roger B. Chaffee burn to death during a launch drill of *Apollo I* at Cape Kennedy, Florida.

July 23: Black inner-city neighborhoods erupt in riots in Detroit, killing forty people and injuring two thousand. Five thousand are left homeless.

October 2: Thurgood Marshall becomes the first African American Supreme Court justice of the United States.

1968

January 30: North Vietnamese and Vietcong troops begin attacks in Vietnam during the Tet Offensive, temporarily overwhelming many U.S.-held positions. Camera crews send pictures of bitter fighting home daily via satellite. Public support for the war declines from 62 percent to 41 percent.

March 16: U.S. troops from Charlie Company savagely massacre between two and six hundred civilians, almost all women, infants, children, and elderly, in the Vietnamese village of My Lai. The tragedy is covered up until late 1969, when helicopter door-gunner Ron Ridenhour writes letters to U.S. senators and representatives.

March 31: President Johnson pulls back bombing of North Vietnam and announces he will not seek or accept reelection.

April 4: Dr. Martin Luther King Jr. is assassinated in Memphis, Tennessee. Riots erupt in 125 cities.

May 10: Paris peace talks begin between the United States and North Vietnam.

May: Students are joined by workers in a general strike that shuts down most of Paris and many other French university towns as the international student movement gains support across the globe, from Prague to Mexico City to Cape Town.

June 5: Democratic presidential candidate and senator Robert F. Kennedy is assassinated as he celebrates his victory in the California primary.

August 28: Chicago police are televised nationally as they viciously attack Festival of Life peace protesters outside the Democratic National Convention.

1969

January 20: Republican Richard M. Nixon becomes the thirty-seventh president of the United States, ending eight years of Democratic presidents.

July 20: The United States wins the space race with Neil Armstrong, the first man to step onto the moon.

March 26: Women stand on their own against the war, organizing a Women Strike for Peace demonstration in Washington, D.C. The group was founded by middle-class housewives who originally went to the Pentagon to talk to those who were ordering their sons into war.

August 15: Woodstock Music Festival draws 500,000 baby boomers—enough for a good-sized city—to a musical camp-out with rock stars on a farm in upstate New York.

October 15: National Vietnam Moratorium launches demonstrations and work stoppages across the United States in a national day of antiwar protest.

November 15: The largest single antiwar demonstration in U.S. history converges more than 250,000 protesters in Washington, D.C.

For Further Reading

Gene Anthony, *Summer of Love.* Millbrae, CA: Celestial Arts, 1980. Photographic journal of Haight-Ashbury in the sixties, with commentary.

Alexander Bloom and Wini Breines, eds., *"Takin' It to the Streets": A Sixties Reader.* New York: Oxford University Press, 1995. A comprehensive anthology of primary documents of representative writings of the sixties. Editors' commentaries provide context for documents and relate them to one another.

Massimo Bonanno, *The Rolling Stones Chronicles.* New York: Henry Holt, 1990. A comprehensive record of "everything that each of the Rolling Stones has ever done from 1960 to the present day." Organized chronologically with an extensive collection of black-and-white photographs.

Peter Bond, *Reaching for the Stars: The Illustrated History of Manned Spaceflight.* London: Cassell, 1993. A comprehensive, well-documented and illustrated look at U.S. and Soviet missions in space, as well as the technology advances and political aspects of space exploration.

Mary Mack Conger, *Sweet Beatle Dreams.* Kansas City, MO: Andrews and McMeel, 1989. An autobiographical diary of a young Beatle fan growing up in the sixties.

Valérie-Anne Giscard d'Estang, *The World Almanac Book of Inventions.* New York: World Almanac Publications, 1985. Descriptions of over two thousand inventions that "changed the world," with interesting information about their inventors, sales, distribution, and impact on society.

Edwin O. Guthman and C. Richard Allen, eds., *RFK Collected Speeches.* New York: Viking, 1993. Chronologically arranged collection of Robert Kennedy's speeches from 1955 through June 4, 1968, edited and introduced by Guthman, Pulitzer Prize–winning journalist and confidant of RFK, and Allen, who worked on RFK's presidential campaign.

Alex Haley and Malcolm X, *The Autobiography of Malcolm X.* New York: Grove Press, 1964. The author of *Roots* cowrites the best-selling "autobiography" of this controversial Black Muslim leader.

Tim Healey, *Picture History of the 20th Century—The Sixties.* London: Franklin Watts, 1988. An English photographic view of key elements of international sixties pop cultural trends.

David Press, *Perspectives: A Multicultural Portrait of America's Music*. New York: Marshall Cavendish, 1994. An engaging and insightful overview of the history of popular music in the United States; well illustrated.

Carl Sagan, *Pale Blue Dot: A Vision of the Human Future in Space*. New York: Random House, 1994. This sequel to the Pulitzer Prize–winning author's best-seller *Cosmos* attempts to show "how science has revolutionized our understanding of where we stand and who we are." Excellent color photographs.

Richard Williams, *Dylan: A Man Called Alias*. New York: Henry Holt, 1992. A richly illustrated, coffee-table-sized biography of Bob Dylan's life, times, friendships, and associates.

Jules Witcover, *The Year the Dream Died: Revisiting 1968 in America*. New York: Warner Books, 1997. A history of the most pivotal year of the decade by a nationally known syndicated journalist.

David Wright, *America in the 20th Century 1960–1969*. New York: Marshall Cavendish, 1995. Sixth in a series of factual, well-illustrated books about the United States in the twentieth century, for teen readers.

Kathy A. Zahler and Diane Zahler, *Test Your Countercultural Literacy*. New York: Arco, Simon & Schuster, 1989. Ten tests of sixties counterculture, grouped by subjects ranging from background issues and events to lifestyles. Provides extensive sixties information in a lighthearted style in answer keys.

Works Consulted

Books

Michael R. Beschloss, ed., *Taking Charge: The Johnson White House Tapes, 1963–64.* New York: Simon and Schuster, 1997. Transcribed tapes of Johnson's private conversations from his first days in office, edited with commentary by a regular commentator on current events on the *Lehrer News Hour,* whom *Newsweek* calls "America's leading historian."

————, *Mayday: Eisenhower, Khrushchev, and the U-2 Affair.* New York: Harper & Row, 1986. An insightful book covering cold war events.

Taylor Branch, *Parting the Waters: America in the King Years 1954–63.* New York: Simon and Schuster, 1988. Winner of the Pulitzer Prize for history, part one of a planned trilogy that chronicles the civil rights movement.

————, *Pillar of Fire: America in the King Years 1963–65.* New York: Simon and Schuster, 1998. Part two of a trilogy based on fifteen years of research, including archival investigation, over two thousand interviews, and new primary sources that range from FBI wiretaps to

White House telephone recordings.

William B. Breuer, *Race to the Moon: America's Duel with the Soviets.* Westport, CT: Praeger, 1993. Covers the thirty-year saga of international competition in the development of rocket science and space technology that culminated in the race to the moon.

Glenn Capp, *The Great Society: A Sourcebook of Speeches.* Belmont, CA: Dickenson, 1967. Texts of speeches from presidents and others on subjects of the Great Society, civil rights, education, and poverty, with notes on context and persuasiveness.

Edward B. Claflin, ed., *JFK Wants to Know: Memos from the President's Office, 1961–1963.* Preface by Pierre Salinger. New York: William Morrow, 1991. An edited collection of presidential memos.

Edward Jay Epstein, *Inquest: The Warren Commission and the Establishment of Truth.* New York: Viking, 1966. A detailed look at the Warren Commission's investigation into the assassination of President Kennedy.

James Farmer, *Freedom—When?* New York: Random House, 1965. The national director of the Congress for

Racial Equality (CORE) discusses problems facing the civil rights movement.

Betty Friedan, *The Feminine Mystique*. New York: Random House, 1963. The book that rekindled the women's movement in the sixties.

————, *It Changed My Life*. New York: Random House, 1976. Writings on the women's movement, 1949–1976.

Goldie Friede and Sue Weiner, *Beatles A to Z*. New York: Methuen, 1980. Dictionary of Beatle information, with extensive black-and-white photograph sections on Beatles collectively, individually, on tour and television; includes their album covers.

Frank B. Gibney and George J. Feldman, *The Reluctant Space-Farers*. New York: The New American Library of World Literature, 1965. Cochairs of the House of Representatives Select Committee on Space and Astronautics in 1958 discuss why "we are in danger of losing history's greatest frontier—not to an alien power but because of our own inertia and lack of foresight."

Todd Gitlin, *The Sixties: Years of Hope, Days of Rage*. New York: Bantam Books, 1987. A somewhat uneven and often personal but well-researched history of the political New Left in the sixties.

J. Evetts Haley, *A Texan Looks at Lyndon: A Study in Illegitimate Power*. Canyon, TX: Palo Duro Press, 1964. A Texan voice from the sixties assesses President Johnson on the basis of his political record and then-current position.

John Hannah, Chairman, *1961 U.S. Civil Rights Commission on Justice Report*. Washington, DC: U.S. Government Printing Office, 1961. A report on police brutality and "private" violence, 1943–1961.

Michael Harrington, *The Other America: Poverty in the United States*. New York: MacMillan, 1962. One of the most influential books of the sixties; a detailed description of poverty's scope and causes.

James Haskins and Kathleen Benson, *The 60s Reader*. New York: Viking Kestrel, 1988. A selection of writings on key issues of the sixties, from movements within the hippie counterculture to civil rights.

Thomas Hauser, with the cooperation of Muhammad Ali, *Muhammad Ali: His Life and Times*. New York: Simon and Schuster, 1991. An insightful biography of the prizefighter-poet, with transcribed interviews.

David Hinckley and Debra Rodman, *The Rolling Stones: Black and White Blues, 1963*. Photographs by Gus

Coral. Atlanta: Turner, 1995. An extensive photographic journal-memoir of the Rolling Stones' 1963 tour, with interviews and history.

Erlend A. Kennan and Edmund H. Harvey Jr., *Mission to the Moon: A Critical Examination of NASA and the Space Program*. New York: William Morrow, 1969. An exploration of the conflict between NASA's charter (which limited it to the peaceful exploration of space) and its relationship to the Department of Defense.

Paul Light, *Baby Boomers*. New York: W. W. Norton, 1988. An insightful study of this influential generation.

Will A. Linkugel, ed., *Contemporary American Speeches: A Sourcebook of Speech Forms and Principles*. Belmont, CA: Wadsworth, 1972. Text of speeches from American presidents and other key players in national life of the United States.

Ernest R. May and Philip D. Zelikow, eds., *The Kennedy Tapes: Inside the White House During the Cuban Missile Crisis*. Cambridge, MA: Belknap Press of Harvard University Press, 1997. Transcripts of recordings from October 1962 released by the JFK Library, with an introduction and scene descriptions preceding each chapter, followed by commentary on what happened after the Cuban missile crisis and lessons

drawn from it.

William F. Melberg, *Moon Missions: Mankind's First Voyages to Another World*. Plymouth, MI: Plymouth Press, 1997. A detailed and concise account of the moon missions of the United States, with black-and-white photographs.

D. Quinn Mills, *Not Like Our Parents*. New York: William Morrow, 1987. A description and examination of differences between the baby boom generation and their parents.

James Olson and Randy Roberts, *Where the Domino Fell: America and Vietnam, 1945–1990*. New York: St. Martin's Press, 1991. A thoughtful study of cold war politics and thought guiding U.S. policy in Vietnam after World War II.

Neil Sheehan, *A Bright and Shining Lie: John Paul Vann and America in Vietnam*. New York: Vintage, 1988. A biography of an American lieutenant colonel in the Vietnam War describes and defines the reasons the United States ultimately lost that war.

Edward Sorel, *Making the World Safe for Hypocrisy*. Chicago: Swallow Press, 1972. A collection of satiric drawings and commentaries by Edward Sorel, many of which were published in national magazines throughout the sixties.

George Sullivan, *The Story of the Peace Corps*. Introduction by Sargent Shriver. New York: Fleet, 1964. A revealing picture of how the Peace Corps came into being, and how it was viewed during its early years.

Harris Wofford, *Of Kennedys and Kings: Making Sense of the Sixties*. Pittsburgh: University of Pittsburgh Press, 1980. A well-indexed memoir of the sixties by Kennedy's special assistant for civil rights, who also cofounded the Peace Corps and arranged King's first meeting with Gandhi. With an introduction by Bill Moyers.

Documents

101st Congress, 1st Session, Senate Document 101-10, *Inaugural Addresses of the Presidents of the United States, from George Washington 1789 to George Bush 1989*. Bicentennial Edition. Washington DC: U.S. Government Printing Office, 1989. Written text of presidential speeches.

Productivity and Poverty. Racine, WI: Johnson Foundation, 1966. A proceedings book of a 1966 Johnson Foundation conference on poverty in the United States.

Index

ABC, 45, 101
Abel, Rudolph, 17
abortion, 89
abstract expressionist
  movement, 93
Accelerated Public Works Act
  of 1962, 36
acid rock, 110
affirmative action, 72
Affluent Society, The, 34
AFL-CIO, 88
African Americans
  annual wages of, 30
  as subject of television
    shows, 102–103
  as subject of theatrical
    productions, 97
  civil rights movement and,
    10, 58–60, 63–64, 67, 71, 74
  Democratic Party's support
    of, 9
  first Supreme Court justice, 72
  joins counterculture, 86
  support of President
    Kennedy, 23–25
  voting rights and, 30–31
Afros, 78
age discrimination, 49
Agent Orange, 45
AIM. *See* American Indian
  Movement
Air Force One, 119
Alabama, 62, 65, 70
Alcatraz, 88–89
Aldrin, Edwin E. "Buzz", Jr.,
  117–19
Ali, Muhammad, 76
Allen, C. Richard, 37
Allen, Steve, 101
Alpert, Richard, 82–83
American Bandstand,
  103–104
American Dream, 71

American Indian Movement
  (AIM), 88
American Indians, 7, 77, 84,
  86, 88
Anders, William A., 116
Andrews, Julie, 100
Animals, 105
Anthony, Gene, 82, 84
antiwar demonstrations, 4, 7,
  43–44, 48, 50–53, 77
Anusziewicz, Richard, 93
apartheid, 61
Apollo 11, 117–18
Apollo program, 113, 115, 120
Archie and Veronica, 99
Area Redevelopment
  Administration, 36
Argentina, 22
Armies of the Night, The, 99
arms race, 12
Armstrong, Neil, 117–19
arts, 9
assassinations, 10, 56, 74–75
atomic weapons, 6, 15, 21, 42

baby boom, 89
baby boomers, 7–8, 39–40,
  48, 54, 77, 79–80, 84–85,
  103, 106, 109
Baez, Joan, 107–108
Ball, Lucille, 101
ballads, 107
Ballard, Hank, 104
ballet, 9
ballistic missiles, 115
Bancroft, Anne, 100
Banks, Dennis, 88
Bay of Pigs invasion, 18, 21
BBC, 105
Be Here Now, 83
be-ins, 94, 109
Beat generation, 80, 86, 99
Beatlemania, 105

Beatles, 80, 83, 95, 105–107,
  110
beatniks, 80
bebop music, 80
Beckwith, Byron de la, 68–69
Bell Telephone, 53, 102, 121
Bellancourt, Clyde, 88
Berlin Wall, 19
Berry, Chuck, 105
Beschloss, Michael, 15
Beverly Hillbillies, The, 101
Bewitched, 101
Birmingham, 25, 65–66, 70
black beat, 109
Black Muslims, 75–76
Black Panthers, 76–77
blacks. *See* African Americans
blues music, 103
Bobby McGee, 110
Bolivia, 22
bomb threats, 68
Bonanza, 101
Borman, Frank, 116
Bosnia, 10
Branch, Taylor, 61
Brazil, 22
Bread and Puppet Theater, 96
Brennan, William J., 72
Breuer, William B., 119
British Invasion, 104–107
Broadway, 97–98
Brown, James, 109
Brown, Linda, 58
Brown v. Board of Education,
  58–59, 72
Buddhists, 45
burning of churches, 70
Burroughs, William, 86
bus boycott in Montgomery,
  62–63, 68

cable television, 45
California, 82, 87

California surfer music, 103
Calm Center, 85
Cambodia, 56
Camelot, 26
Cameo–Parkway Records, 104
Campbell's soup, 93
Canada, 48
cancer, 15
Candid Camera, 101
Cannes Film Festival, 97
Caroll, Diahann, 102
Carter, Jimmy, 10
Castro, Fidel, 17–18
Catch 22, 99
Catholics, 45
CBS, 45, 47, 72, 101
Central Intelligence Agency
  (CIA), 16, 20, 43
Chaffee, Roger, 117
chanting, 98–99
Charles, Ray, 109
Chavez, Cesar, 87–88
Checker, Chubby, 103–104
Checkpoint Charlie, 19
chemical warfare, 42, 45
Chicanos, 7, 77, 88
Chicken, 103
Chile, 22
China, 42
Chisholm, Shirley, 91
church burnings, 70
Church, Frank, 48
CIA. *See* Central Intelligence
  Agency
Civil Rights Acts of 1964 and
  1965, 31–32, 36, 74
civil rights movement, 10,
  23–25, 29–30, 35, 57–78,
  86, 90–91
Civil War, 10, 58, 66–67
Clark, Dick, 103, 105, 107
Clay, Cassius. *See* Ali,
  Muhammad
cocaine, 82
COFO. *See* Council of
  Federated Organizations
Cohen, Allen, 82
cold war, 6, 12–23, 42

colleges, 39–40
college students, 77–78
College Work-Study Program,
  32–33
Collins, Michael, 119
Colombia, 22
color television, 45
Columbia University, 78
comedy shows, 102
comic strips, 93
communal living, 8
communism
  Berlin Wall as symbol of, 19
  efforts to free Cuba from,
    17–23
  fight against in Vietnam, 41–42
  McCarthyism and, 5
  practice of by Soviet Union, 13
  religious persecution by, 45
computers, 121
Congress for Racial Equality
  (CORE), 62, 64
Connally, John, 26
*Contemporary American
  Speeches,* 50
CORE. *See* Congress for Racial
  Equality
corn rows, 78
Costa Rica, 22
Council of Federated
  Organizations (COFO), 58
countercultures, 79–92, 106,
  109
Country Joe and the Fish, 8
country music, 103
Credentials Committee, 69
credibility gap, 49
Cronkite, Walter, 47, 72
Crumb, R., 99
Cuba, 17–23
Cuban missile crisis, 20–21

Dallas, 26
dances, 103
dashikis, 78
Dass, Ram, 83
Davis, Angela, 91
Davis, R. G., 96

Davis, Sammy, Jr., 103
DC 9, 51–52
death penalty, 72
Dee, Joey, 104
Defense Department, 115
Democratic National
  Convention, 9–10, 48, 69
Democratic Party, 9–10
demonstrations
  against war, 4, 7, 43–44, 48,
    50–53, 91, 99
  as basic freedom, 10
  for civil rights, 25, 57,
    61–62, 65, 71, 73
  in London, 107
  Poor People's March, 28
  use of nonviolence in, 10,
    25, 77
Diana Ross and the Supremes,
  109
Diddley, Bo, 105
Diem, Ngo Dinh, 41, 43
Digger Papers, The, 85
Diggers, 85
Digital Equipment
  Corporation, 121
Diller, Phyllis, 103
discrimination, 24, 31, 49, 74
disposable dresses, 94
Dominican Republic, 22
domino theory, 42, 44
Dow Chemical, 51–53, 78
draft cards, 48–49
dress codes, 80
*Dr. Strangelove: How I Learned
  to Stop Worrying and Love the
  Bomb,* 99–100
drugs, 40, 80–85, 110
Dugger, Ronnie, 30
Dylan, Bob, 4, 107–108

Eagle, 117–18
East Germany, 19
Echo I, 120
Economic Opportunity Act,
  31, 36
Ecuador, 22
Ed Sullivan Show, 80

education, 33–35, 39–40, 58–60
Eisenhower, Dwight D. 6, 15–17, 42–43, 61
elections, 41–42, 67–68
electrification, 30
El Salvador, 22
El Teatro Campesino, 96
Evers, Medgar, 10, 68
Explorer I, 112

Fabares, Shelley, 107
Family Affair, 101
Fang, 103
Farad, Wali, 75–76
Farmer, James, 25, 62
farming, 45
farm price supports, 30
fashion, 93–94
FBI. *See* Federal Bureau of Investigation
Federal Bureau of Investigation (FBI), 48, 70–72, 75, 77
Feldman, George B., 116
Feminine Mystique, The, 89–90
feminism, 91
fiddle tunes, 107
fine arts, 9
finger cymbals, 99
Finger Poppin' Time, 104
flower power, 8
folk music, 103, 107–108
Foreign Relations Committee of the U.S. Senate, 50
Fourteenth Amendment, 32
Franklin, Aretha, 109
Freedom Ride Campaign, 65
Freedom Riders, 61, 65–67
Freedom Vote of 1963, 68
Freedom—When?, 62
Free Speech movement, 6, 9
French-Indochina War, 40–41
Friedan, Betty, 89–90
Friendship 7, 115
Fritz the Cat, 99
Frug, 103

Fulbright, J. William, 48

Gagarin, Yuri, 112
Galbraith, J. K., 34
Gandhi, Mahatma, 25, 61, 77
Garson, Barbara, 96
General Electric, 53
generation gap, 48–49
Germany, 12, 19
Giant Hamburger, The, 95
Gibney, Frank, 116
Ginsberg, Allen, 98
Gleason, Jackie, 101
Glenn, John H., Jr., 115
Glover, Henry, 104
Goldwater, Barry, 44
Gordy, Berry, Jr., 109
gospel music, 103, 105, 109
Graduate, The, 100
Graham, Billy, 61
Grapefruit, 95
Great Depression, 34, 36
Great Society, 28–31, 36, 38, 54
Green Berets, The, 100
Greensboro, 61
Greyhound, 65, 84
Griffith, Andy, 101
Grissom, Gus, 117
Guatemala, 22
guerrilla theater, 96, 98
Gulf of Tonkin Resolution, 43
Gulf War, 10
Guthman, Edwin O., 37

Haight-Ashbury district, 81–82, 84–85, 97
Hair, 97
haircuts, 80, 93
Haiti, 22
Haley, Bill, 105
hallucinations, 82
Hamer, Fannie Lou, 69
Hansberry, Lorraine, 97
happenings, 94–95
Hard Day's Night, A, 105
Harrington, Michael, 34
Harvey, Edmund H., Jr., 114
Hawn, Goldie, 101–102

Head Comix, 99
Head Start, 10, 32, 35–36
helium-3, 120
Heller, Joseph, 99
Help!, 105
Hendrix, Jimi, 8, 109–10
Hepburn, Audrey, 100
heroin, 82
hippies, 8, 79–82, 84–86, 92, 94, 97–98
Hiroshima, 6, 21
Hispanics, 77, 86
Hit Parade, 108
Hitchhiker, 103
hitchhiking, 85
Ho Chi Minh City, 56
Hoffman, Abbie, 7, 47
Hoffman, Dustin, 100
Holly, Buddy, 105, 107
Honduras, 22
Hoover, Erna Schneider, 121
Hoover, J. Edgar, 27, 70–71, 75
Hornet, 119
House Judiciary Committee, 25
House Rules Committee, 25
House Select Committee on Assassinations, 75
House Subcommittee on NASA Oversight, 114
Howl, 99
Humphrey, Hubert, 10, 30–31, 33, 48, 56, 69, 74
Huxley, Aldous, 84

improvisation, 96
India, 61
Indian reservations, 37
Indochina, 42–43
integration, 59, 62–65, 73
invisible poor, 34
Itta Bena (Mississippi), 71
Izvestia, 70

Jackson, Jesse, 74
Jackson Five, The, 109
Japan, 6, 21
jazz music, 80, 103, 105
Jerk, 103

Jim Crow laws, 58, 63, 74
Job Corps, 32
Joey Dee and the Starliters, 104
"Johnny Angel," 107
Johnson, Arte, 102
Johnson, Lady Bird, 26, 96
Johnson, Lyndon Baines
  as subject of theatrical
    productions, 96
  presidency of
    appoints first African
      American Supreme Court
      justice, 72
    approves wiretaps on
      Martin Luther King, 75
    civil rights and, 69–71, 74
    convinces Congress to pass
      Medicare bill, 35
    efforts to fight poverty, 9,
      28–33, 36
    support of education by, 33
    Vietnam War and, 36, 39–56
    sworn in as president, 26
Joplin, Janis, 110
Judaism, 99
Julia, 102
Justice Department, 23, 70

Kaddish and Other Poems
  1958–60, 99
Kaprow, Allan, 94
Kennan, Erlend A., 114
Kennedy, Jacqueline (Jackie)
  Bouvier, 26
Kennedy, John F.
  as subject of theatrical
    productions, 96
  death of, 10, 26, 75
  presidency of
    announces Proclamation of
      Quarantine, 22
    approves wiretaps on
      Martin Luther King, 75
    Bay of Pigs invasion and,
      18, 21
    comments of about
      poverty, 29
    Cuban missile crisis and,

20–21
    efforts to avoid nuclear
      war, 6
    inherits Vietnam War,
      42–43
    meeting with during March
      on Washington, 64
    orders standoff at
      Checkpoint Charlie, 19
    popularity of, 23–25
    support of the arts by, 9
    support of Peace Corps by,
      32–33
    support for space
      exploration, 112–17
    stops violence in
      Montgomery, 66
Kennedy, Robert, 9, 10, 20,
  23, 37, 54–56, 70, 74–75, 87
Kennedy, Ted, 23
Kerouac, Jack, 99
Kerry, John F., 50
Kesey, Ken, 99
Keyes v. School District No. 1 of
  Denver, 72
Khrushchev, Nikita S., 13,
  15–19, 22–23
Kilby, Jack, 121
King, Martin Luther, Jr.,
  10–11, 25, 29, 57, 61–64,
  68, 73–75
Kiowa Indians, 84
Kissinger, Henry, 9
Kodak color film, 45
Korea, 6
Korry, Edward, 25
Kovacs, Ernie, 101

Laugh-In, 101–102
Lawrence of Arabia, 99
Leary, Timothy, 82–83
Lee, Harper, 99
leisure suits, 93
Lennon, John, 95
Let It Be, 105
levitating the Pentagon, 52
Lichtenstein, Roy, 93
Life, 82–83

Limbo, 103
Lincoln, Abraham, 24
Lincoln Memorial, 25, 64
Lindbergh law, 70
Linkugal, Will A., 50
Little Richard, 105, 107
Living Theater, The, 96
Los Angeles, 74
"Lose Your Inhibitions Twist,
  The," 104
Louisiana, 59
Love, John, 89
love songs, 107
Lovell, James A., Jr., 116
Lowenstein, Allard, 67–68
LSD, 8, 82–83, 93–94, 98
Luizzo, Viola, 73
Luna 9, 116
Luna 10, 116
lynching, 30
lysergic acid diethylamide. See
  LSD

Macbeth, 96
MacBird!, 96
Magical Mystery Tour, 105
Mailer, Norman, 99
Malcolm X, 10, 75–76
Manned Spacecraft Center, 119
March on Washington, 25, 57,
  62, 64, 70
marijuana, 8, 80–82, 94, 98
Mariner 2, 116
Mars 1, 116
Marshall, Thurgood, 72
Martin, Dick, 101–102
Mashed Potatoes, 103
Max, Peter, 93
McCarthy, Eugene, 9, 53
McCarthy, Joseph, 5
McCarthyism, 5, 9
Medicaid, 10
Medicare, 10, 35–36
meditation, 83–84, 98
Memphis, 74
Mercury, 112
Meredith, James, 59–60
mescaline, 80, 82

Mexican Americans, 87
See also Chicanos
Mexico, 22
MIA. *See* Montgomery
  Improvement Association
migrant workers, 77, 87
Minh, Ho Chi, 41, 45
miniskirts, 93–94
Mississippi, 69–72
"Mississippi: A Foreign
  Country in Our Midst?", 68
mock election, 68
Monroe, Marilyn, 93
Monterey Folk Festival, 108
Montgomery, 66, 73
Montgomery bus boycott,
  62–63, 68
Montgomery Improvement
  Association (MIA), 62
Moon Missions, 120
mop, 80, 106
Moses, Robert (Bob), 57–58, 72
Motor City Comics, 99
Motown, 103, 108–109
movies, 99–101
"Mrs. Robinson," 100
Muddy Waters, 105
Muhammad, Elijah, 76
*Muhammad Ali: His Life and
  Times,* 76
Murrow, Edward R., 9
Museum of Modern Art, 93
music, 80, 97, 103–10
mutton chops, 93
mutual deterrent, 15
My Fair Lady, 100
My Lai, 50

NAACP. *See* National
  Association for the
  Advancement of Colored
  People
Nagasaki, 6, 21
Naked Lunch, 86
napalm, 42, 51
NASA, 114, 117
National Association for the
  Advancement of Colored

People (NAACP), 10, 63, 68,
  72
National Defense Education
  Act of 1958, 39
National Farm Workers
  Association (NFWA), 88
National Guard, 74
National Security Council, 6
NATO. *See* North Atlantic
  Treaty Organization
Navajo Indians, 84
Nazi Germany, 12
NBC, 45, 101
Nehru jackets, 94
Nehru, Jawaharlal, 94
Neighborhood Youth Corps, 32
Neshoba County, 70
Neville, Richard, 99
New Deal, 36
New Left, 7, 10, 85–86
New York, 93
New York City, 119
New York Drama Critics'
  Circle Award, 97
New York Times, 70–71
news, 45, 47–48, 71–72
news cycle, 7
Newton, Huey, 76
NFWA. *See* National Farm
  Workers Association
Nicaragua, 22
nicotine, 82
Nixon, Richard M., 9–10, 56,
  77, 118–19
nonviolence, 10, 25, 61–62,
  64, 65, 77, 87
North Atlantic Treaty
  Organization (NATO), 22
North Carolina, 61
North Vietnam, 41–43, 45,
  53, 55–56
novelists, 99
nuclear war, 6, 14–15, 20, 44
nuclear weapons, 18, 21, 116
nudity, 97

OAS. *See* Organization of
  American States

observatories in space, 116
O'Connor, Eugene ("Bull"), 70
Office of Economic
  Opportunity, 32
*Of Kennedys and Kings: Making
  Sense of the Sixties,* 25, 75
Oldenburg, Claes, 94–95
Olson, James, 6, 43
*One Flew Over the Cuckoo's
  Nest,* 99
Only a Pawn in Their Game, 108
Ono, Yoko, 95
Op art, 93–94
opera, 9
orchestras, 9
Organization of Afro-
  Americans, 76
Organization of American
  States (OAS), 22
OSO-1, 116
Oswald, Lee Harvey, 26–27
Other America, The, 34
overtime, 30

Panama, 22
Paraguay, 22
Parchman Penitentiary, 61
Parks, Rosa, 62–63
patriotism, 40
Patton, 99
payola, 107
Peace Corps, 25, 32–33
peaceful coexistence, 13
Pearl River, 72
Pentagon, 49, 52
Peppermint Twist, 104
Peru, 22
peyote, 84
Philadelphia (Mississippi), 72
Philadelphia sound, 109
pill, the, 89–90
Pillar of Fire, 70
Plessy v. Ferguson, 58
poetry, 95, 98–99
Poitier, Sidney, 97
poll tax, 30, 67–68, 73
Pony, 103
Poor People's March, 28

populism, 5
poverty, 9, 28–37, 40, 58
Powers, Francis Gary, 16–17
pregnancy, 89
Presley, Elvis, 104–105, 107
Price, Cecil, 70, 73
progressive jazz music, 80
protests
  against war, 4, 7, 43–44, 48,
    50–53, 91, 99
  as basic freedom, 10
  for civil rights, 25, 57,
    61–62, 65, 71, 73
  in London, 107
  Poor People's March, 28
  use of nonviolence in, 10,
    25, 77
public works projects, 36
Pulitzer Prize, 99

Race to the Moon: America's
  Duel with the Soviets, 119
racism, 29–30, 34, 40, 76–78,
  91
radiation sickness, 15
Rado, James, 97
Ragni, Gerome, 97
Rainey, Lawrence, 70, 72
Raisin in the Sun, 97
RAM. See random-access
  memory
Randolph, A. Philip, 25
random-access memory
  (RAM), 121
Rawhide, 101
Ray, James Earl, 74–75
reading tests, 67–68, 73
Red menace, 5
Reeb, James, 73
religious persecution, 45
Republican Party, 9
RFK Collected Speeches, 37, 87
rhythm and blues music, 103,
  105, 107
rice, 45
Richards, Keith, 105
rights of criminal defendants,
  72

Riley, Bridget, 93
riots, 74–75, 110
Roberts, Randy, 6, 43
rock 'n' roll music, 8, 97,
  103–107
rock-a-billy music, 103
Rolling Stones, 105, 107
Rolling Stones, The, 105
Roosevelt, Franklin Delano, 36
Rowan, Dan, 101–102
Rubin, Jerry, 47, 52
Ruby, Jack, 26–27

Sacramento, 87
Safer, Morley, 45
Sagan, Carl, 112, 118
Saigon, 40, 56
Samaras, Lucas, 94–95
sandals, 94
San Francisco, 84–85, 88
San Francisco Mime Troupe,
  96–97
satellites, 44–45, 112, 115, 120
Schmitt, Harrison H., 120
Schumann, Peter, 96
SDS. See Students for a
  Democratic Society
Sea of Tranquility, 117–18
Seale, Bobby, 76
Second Emancipation
  Proclamation, 24
Seeger, Pete, 108
segregation, 58–59, 61,
  65–70, 72–74, 78
Sellers, Peter, 99
Selma, 73
Senate, 50
sex, 40, 89
Shakespeare, 96
Shepard, Alan B. Jr., 112
Shriver, Sargent, 25, 33
sideburns, 93
Silent Generation, 5
Simon and Garfunkel, 100
Sioux Indians, 89
Sirhan, Sirhan Bishara, 55
sit-ins, 61, 71, 94
Sixteenth Street Baptist

Church, 25
Skelton, Red, 101
Slaughterhouse Five, 99
slavery, 57–58
Slop, 103
Sly and Family Stone, 109
Smokey Robinson and the
  Miracles, 109
Smothers Brothers, The, 101, 102
SNCC. See Student Nonviolent
  Coordinating Committee
socialism, 5
Social Security, 30
Soft Fur Good Humors, 95
soft sculpture, 95
soul music, 103, 105, 109
Sound of Music, The, 99–100
South Africa, 61
South Vietnam, 41–45, 49, 56
Soviet Union
  involvement of in cold war,
    12–23
  space exploration and,
    111–12, 116
  support of North Vietnam, 42
space exploration, 111–21
Sputnik I, 112
Stock Exchange, 7
Store, The, 95
"Street Fighting Man," 107
street theater, 96, 98
Stroll, 105
strychnine, 82
Student Nonviolent
  Coordinating Committee
  (SNCC), 65, 67, 69
Students for a Democratic
  Society (SDS), 7, 44
suicide, 37
Sullivan, Ed, 101
Summer of Love, 82, 98
Sunnie, Jeff, 69
superpowers, 12
Supreme Court, 58, 62, 72
Swim, 103

"Takin' It to the Streets," 69
Tang®, 120

taxes, 29, 37
teach-in movement, 40
Teamsters Union, 73
telephone switches, 121
television, 7, 44–45, 47–48, 71–72, 98, 101–103
Tennessee, 74
Tereshkova, Valentina, 116
test-ban treaty, 116
Tet offensive, 53, 55
Texas, 26
Texas Instruments, 121
Texas Observer, 30
theater, 96, 98
"The Doors of Perception," 84
"The Johnson Record—II," 30
Thomas, Danny, 101
Times They Are A-Changin', The, 108
TM. *See* transcendental meditation
To Kill a Mockingbird, 99
tobacco, 81–82
Tomlin, Lily, 101–102
Trailways, 65
transcendental meditation (TM), 83–84
treaty rights, 88
Tuscaloosa, 23
Twenty-sixth Amendment, 49
Twist, 103–104

U-2 spy planes, 15–16
unemployment, 30, 36–37
Union of Soviet Socialist Republics (USSR). *See* Soviet Union
unions, 30
United Nations, 22, 116
United States
  civil rights movement in, 10, 23–25, 29–30, 35, 57–78
  efforts of to free Cuba from communism, 17–23
  involvement of in cold war, 6, 12–23
  space exploration and, 111–20
  standoff at Checkpoint

Charlie, 19
  Vietnam War and, 6–7, 10, 36, 38, 39–56
University of Alabama, 24, 59
University of Mississippi, 60
Uruguay, 22
U.S. Air Force, 16
U.S. Constitution, 32, 43, 62, 67
U.S. Department of Defense, 52
U.S. National Guard, 7, 19
U.S. Senate, 50
USSR. *See* Soviet Union

Valens, Richie, 107
Van Dyke, Dick, 101
Vann, John Paul, 46
Vasarely, Victor, 93
Velcro®, 120
Venera 1, 116
Venera 3, 116
Venezuela, 22
Venus, 116
veterans of Vietnam, 50
Vietcong, 42, 46, 49–50, 53
Vietnam Veterans Against the War, 50
Vietnam War, 6–7, 10, 36, 38, 39–56, 76–77, 86, 90–91, 96, 101, 110, 118
Vietnamization, 56
VISTA (Volunteers in Service to America), 32, 33
visual arts, 93
Volunteers in Service to America. *See* VISTA
Vonnegut, Kurt, 99
Voskhod 1, 116
Voskhod 2, 116
Vostok 1, 116
Vostok 6, 116
voting rights, 30–31, 58, 63, 67–69, 73–74, 91
Voting Rights Acts, 73–74

Walk Against Fear, 60
Wall Street, 80
Wallace, George, 9, 23, 59
Warhol, Andy, 93

war industry, 6, 29
War on Poverty, 9, 28, 30–32, 86
War on Poverty Act, 31, 36
Washington, D.C.
  antiwar protests in, 4, 91, 99
  March on Washington, 25, 57
  Poor People's March, 28
Washington Monument, 64
Watergate Hotel, 56
Watts riot, 74
Watusi, 103
Wayne, John, 100–101
Wayne, Mike, 101
West Germany, 19
Where Have all the Flowers Gone?, 108
Where the Domino Fell: America and Vietnam, 1945–1990, 6, 43
White, Ed, 117
Whitman, Walt, 99
Who, 105
"With God on Our Side," 108
WLAC (radio station), 104
Wofford, Harris, 25, 75
women's liberation movement, 7, 77, 88–91
Women Strike for Peace, 91
Wonder, Stevie, 109
Woodstock generation. *See* baby boomers
Woodstock music festival, 92, 109–10
World War II, 5–6, 12, 14, 19, 21, 29, 42–43, 45, 53, 99

Yippie. *See* Youth International Party
Yogi, Maharishi Mahesh, 83
Youth International Party (Yippie), 7, 47, 52
Yo-Yo Man, 101

Zaldívar, Fulgencio Batista y, 17
Zapp Comix, 99
Zen Buddhism, 99

Picture Credits

Cover photos (from left to right): Archive Photos, Bettmann, Corbis-Bettmann

American Stock/Archive Photos, 76

AP Wide World Photos, 77, 87

Archive Photos, 5, 16, 34, 41, 49, 92, 95,100, 104, 106, 110, 115, 117

CBS Archives/Archive Photos, 47

Corbis, 102

Deutsche Presse/Archive Photos, 19

Express Newspapers/Archive Photos, 94

Library of Congress, 6, 11, 20, 28, 32, 54, 57, 59, 60, 63, 65

NASA, 111, 113, 119

National Archives, 8, 13, 17, 21, 24, 27, 35, 39, 46, 51, 79

Popperfoto/Archive Photos, 55

Santi Visalli Inc./Archive Photos, 83

UPI Corbis-Bettmann, 4, 12, 73, 81, 84, 89, 90, 97, 98, 108

About the Author

Gini Holland is a consulting teacher for the Milwaukee public school system. Her son Noah Tabakin is the lead singer and saxophone player for "The Little Blue Crunchy Things," a funk rock band managed by her husband, Daniel. Aside from Crunchy music, some of her favorite pleasures in life include international travel, meditation, great friends, her two funny cats, and photography. This is her eighteenth non-fiction book for children and young adults.